AD

ARCHITECTURAL DESIGN

GUEST-EDITED BY
DAVID LITTLEFIELD

LONDON (RE) GENERATION

01|2012

ARCHITECTURAL DESIGN
VOL 82, NO 1
JANUARY/FEBRUARY 2012
ISSN 0003-8504

PROFILE NO 215
ISBN 978-1119-993780

ARCHITECTURAL DESIGN

LONDON (RE) GENERATION

32

*'Cities appear to grow, stagnate, suffer blight,
repair themselves, shift their centres of gravity,
develop a hierarchy of arteries and nodes, and
pulse with activity.' — David Littlefield*

AD

ARCHITECTURAL DESIGN
JANUARY/FEBRUARY 2012
PROFILE NO 215

Editorial Offices
John Wiley & Sons
25 John Street
London
WC1N 2BS

T: +44 (0)20 8326 3800

Editor
Helen Castle

Managing Editor (Freelance)
Caroline Ellerby

Production Editor
Elizabeth Gongde

Prepress
Artmedia, London

Art Direction and Design
CHK Design:
Christian Küsters
Sophie Troppmair

Printed in Italy by Conti Tipocolor

Sponsorship/advertising
Faith Pidduck/Wayne Frost
T: +44 (0)1243 770254
E: fpidduck@wiley.co.uk

Subscribe to AD

AD is published bimonthly and is
available to purchase on both a
subscription basis and as individual
volumes at the following prices.

Prices
Individual copies: £22.99 / US$45
Mailing fees may apply

Annual Subscription Rates
Student: £75 / US$117 print only
Individual: £120 / US$189 print only
Institutional: £200 / US$375 print or
online
Institutional: £230 / US$431 combined
print and online

Subscription Offices UK
John Wiley & Sons Ltd
Journals Administration Department
1 Oldlands Way, Bognor Regis
West Sussex, PO22 9SA
T: +44 (0)1243 843272
F: +44 (0)1243 843232
E: cs-journals@wiley.co.uk

Print ISSN: 0003-8504;
Online ISSN: 1554-2769

Prices are for six issues and include
postage and handling charges.
Individual rate subscriptions must be
paid by personal cheque or credit card.
Individual rate subscriptions may not
be resold or used as library copies.

All prices are subject to change
without notice.

Rights and Permissions
Requests to the Publisher should be
addressed to:
Permissions Department
John Wiley & Sons Ltd
The Atrium
Southern Gate
Chichester
West Sussex PO19 8SQ
England

F: +44 (0)1243 770620
E: permreq@wiley.co.uk

Front cover: Base map © OpenStreetMap.
Image by Eric Fischer.
Inside front cover: Concept CHK Design

EDITORIAL
Helen Castle

When the London 2012 Olympic and Paralympic Games open in July, the enormity of the changes to East London will be as dramatic for any visitor from the West End, who has not recently visited Stratford, as for a tourist from Australia. The Games have involved the construction of new sporting venues, most conspicuously the Velodrome by Hopkins Architects, the Olympic Stadium by Populous and the Aquatics Centre by Zaha Hadid Architects. They have also included extensive new permanent housing in the Olympic and Paralympic Village. Perhaps most far-reaching for the area, though, has been the whole-scale decontamination and cleanup of the Lea Valley which was undertaken before any building work took place. The Games have also facilitated a new level of investment in much-needed infrastructure to East London, with new rail and transport links. They are also leaving in their wake a beautifully landscaped public park – of a size that has not been built since the 19th century.

It was clear that △D should both mark and review the changing face of its home city in 2012. The theme of regeneration has been embraced by guest-editor David Littlefield, who invited an impressive cast of contributors not only to survey the shifts in the metropolis in East London and elsewhere, but also to question the currency of regeneration itself. When so much lip service is paid to the concept of regeneration, there is the very real danger that it is becoming devalued and may come to mean everything and nothing. What is clear, though, is that regeneration remains to be broadly understood as being about positive change – a force for the good – even if there are widely diverging views about the dynamics of this force and the projects that can truly be categorised as regenerative. At a time when private partnerships have become a requirement for any kind of development, at the large scale requiring injections of capital from overseas, commercial concerns have become the driving force. As Murray Fraser so aptly charts in his article (see pages 14–21), global investment has also impacted the nature of development in the capital in recent years. There has been a marked shift from a US model of urbanism to a more global one, influenced by investors from the Middle East, Far East, Russia and Australia. How can this capital be captured/countered to ensure schemes remain regenerative at a local level? Are there existing models of long-term stewardship that can be drawn on in development? How can we keep championing the needs of the periphery or edge, as well as the commercial centre, without the intervention of effective public bodies? △D

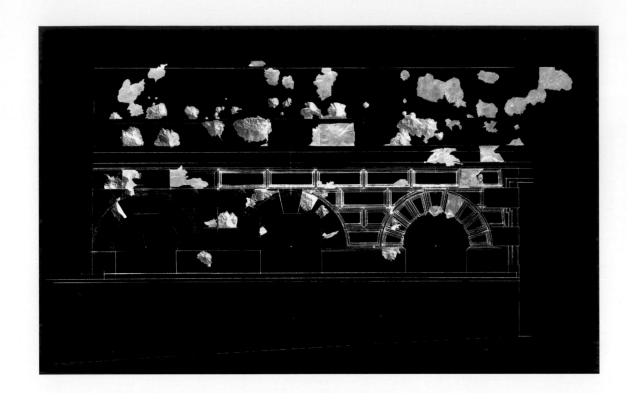

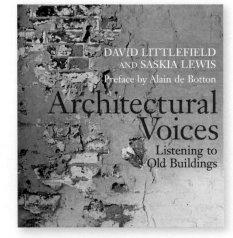

David Littlefield, Tate Britain facade study, Millbank, London, 2007
top: Drawing/photomontage of the gallery's bomb-damaged facade. The unplanned mark-making of the Blitz has become an integral element within the fabric of the building. These marks now go unnoticed by passers-by; their presence is made explicit in this drawing.

Estranged Space, Roman Baths, Bath, England, 2010
above left: The Estranged Space research group is deploying art practice to reinterpret and re-present the vaults beneath York Street; this depiction is a montage of camera obscura images, captured by the vaults, of the heritage zone beyond.

Architectural Voices: Listening to Old Buildings
above: Co-written by David Littlefield and Saskia Lewis, *Architectural Voices* (John Wiley & Sons, 2007) examines the role of narrative when reconsidering buildings for redevelopment, asking how meaning can be found or generated through developing a particular attitude towards place.

David Littlefield is a senior lecturer in the Department of Planning and Architecture at the University of the West of England (UWE), Bristol. He has taught at Chelsea College of Art & Design, and the universities of Bath and Plymouth, and he is an external examiner for the interior architecture programme at Leeds Metropolitan University. He is the author of a number of books, including *Liverpool One: Remaking a City Centre* (John Wiley & Sons, 2010), and co-author of *Architectural Voices: Listening to Old Buildings* (John Wiley & Sons, 2007).

David is a member of a number of professional networks and associations, including Mapping Spectral Traces – a group founded by geographers and artists that seeks to tease out and make evident the ways in which human habitation marks the earth, no matter how faintly. Importantly, the group does not privilege the physical over the non-physical; narrative and memory are as much a part of the study as the stuff of bricks, mortar and hard facts. In a more geographical sense, the work of this network attempts to map what ordinarily goes unmapped; it is a cartography of place in its widest sense, rather than of conventional geophysical points.

The sense of what we mean by 'place' underpins David's work. Place is a term over which no particular discipline has a monopoly; it is an amalgam of subjects as diverse as numerical coordinates and identity, embracing what UNESCO calls the tangible and the intangible when attempting to define another slippery term – 'authenticity'. David is currently exploring these notions with the research group Estranged Space, which has been granted artist in residence status at the Roman Baths in Bath, England. This work involves the use of art practice in order to arrive at a better, or fuller, understanding of a particular space, its significance and the factors that might play a role in its redevelopment.

Further information on David's work and networks can be found at www.estranged_space.net and www.mappingspectraltraces.org. ⌂

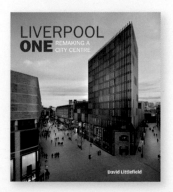

Liverpool One: Remaking a City Centre
Authored by David Littlefield and commissioned by Grosvenor, *Liverpool One* (John Wiley & Sons, 2010) tells the political, commercial, architectural and planning stories behind the retail-led development that has transformed the centre of the city.

(RE)GENERATION:
PLACE, MEMORY, IDENTITY

York Watergate was built in 1626 as a threshold between the Duke of Buckingham's gardens and the river Thames. This elaborate Italianate structure, perhaps designed by Inigo Jones, was one of many water gates and river stairs along the northern bank of the Thames, then flanked by the residences of the rich and powerful. Today, this rusticated gateway is landlocked, located 137 metres (449 feet) from the water's edge; staggeringly, it is not the gateway that has moved, but the river. Nothing remains of the house and garden, which were demolished and replaced by a new street pattern in 1675, although the duke's name (George Villiers) survives in Villiers Street, which connects Victoria Embankment with the Strand. Indeed, the Strand (Saxon for beach or shore) marked the northern edge of the Thames in even earlier times; so Joseph Bazalgette's monumental embankment project, which marooned the York Watergate when completed in 1874, is merely the latest in a series of moves that have shifted the positions of land and water in Central London. This gate, now a folly, is emblematic of profound change, which is still a condition of London. But the gate is more than a folly – it is the embodiment of urban memory, a monument not just to the past, but to notions of place.

Cities have often been compared with living organisms, and for good reason. Viewed from above over time, they would appear to grow, stagnate, suffer blight, repair themselves, shift their centres of gravity, develop a hierarchy of arteries and nodes, and pulse with activity. The term 'regeneration', then, would seem appropriate in describing the changes and fixes applied to urban forms when attempting to arrest decay or wrest further value from exhausted or troubled land. The term is certainly suggestive of organic, biological renewal. One must be very careful with language, however, because words can easily disguise true intentions – masking, say, rampant commercialism or manifestations of power as, say, a social good.

Property development is not the same thing as regeneration. Nor is change. Of course, regeneration in the context of the built environment typically embodies change and construction to some extent, but these terms must never be confused as synonyms. Further, we must be a little cautious when considering cities as organisms. Mike Batty, from University College London (UCL), provides a powerful case for the comparison (see pages 54–59), but he is careful to alert us to the limits of the parallel; yes, the city can, like a crowd, be considered as a living entity, and its complex processes can be modelled and predicted with a great deal of accuracy and usefulness. However, we would do well to remember that the city does not actually heal or regenerate itself; it relies on the active agents (people, policy-makers) within that organism to provoke change.

Not that there is anything wrong with change or construction. When the Strand ceased to be a beach and became, instead, a thoroughfare separated from (but parallel to) the Thames, that was not regeneration. The demolition and replacement of the duke of Buckingham's house and garden was not regeneration either. Nor was the creation of Victoria Embankment. These were building projects, conceived out of a mixture of economic gain, social advantage, a need for better transport, improved health and sanitation and so on. The term regeneration is most usefully invoked as part of an attempt to reverse economic decline and social deprivation, a set of actions to restart the processes of generating wealth and providing inhabitants with viable social and economic choices. Property development, or 'urban renewal', might well be the catalyst for these things, but there is always the danger that it becomes a placebo.

Twenty years ago a prestigious planning journal[1] ran a telling paper that charted the fortunes of the well-meaning Glasgow East Area Renewal project, which ran across the 1970s and 1980s. The article recorded the fact that although housing standards and perceptions of the area rose, environmental conditions improved and local people were not priced out of the area through processes of gentrification, there was still no noticeable effect on economic decline and employment prospects; and where new jobs were created, these were often filled by commuters who lived elsewhere. This is now a very real question for East London's Stratford; once the London 2012 Olympic and Paralympic Games have come and gone, and this vast estate has been reworked, how can we be sure that any wealth generated will stay in the area and not be sucked westwards, leaving the area transformed but little better for the people who have lived there for many years? This outcome is a real possibility, as is demonstrated on pages 54–59. 'The danger in the early 21st century is not that regeneration through the engines of casinos, conventions and coliseums might displace communities – but that it might simply ignore them,' wrote Susan Batty in 2003.[2]

Murray Fraser writes (see pages 14–21) of the global forces, both economic and architectural, which are increasingly

George Frederick Cruchley, *Cruchley's New Plan of London and its Environs*, 1828
centre: This map shows the new Royal Parks and is drawn at a larger scale than earlier maps, illustrating the city's potential for growth.

John Rocque, *A plan of London with all the new streets*, 1766
bottom: Rocque's plan is based on a survey that began in 1738. Published on 24 sheets, the map is said to be the most accurate of 18th-century London.

defining large-scale enterprises in London. As a global city,
there appears to be a very real question over whether or not
London is a powerful manipulator of these powerful forces
or merely the passive recipient of them. This question has
important consequences for the role of place, and place
making, in the city – that is, the extent to which any sense
of identity or London-ness could or should play in property-
led regeneration programmes. Writing in *City Reborn:
Architecture and Regeneration in London, from Bankside to
Dulwich*, Renzo Piano eloquently describes the context for the
310-metre (1,107-foot) Shard tower, now nearing completion:

> Southwark is one of those places where you can feel the
> layers of history: you can tell how the city has grown
> organically from the morphology of nature, the topography
> of the ground and the curve of the river. The fact is that
> Southwark was never actually designed: it has simply
> grown out of millions of single true lives … Is it possible to
> solve [difficult] problems without betraying the identity of
> these places? I think so.[3]

310 HEIGHT
     IN METRES
     OF SHARD
     TOWER

Despite the tower's merits, Piano's building could be described
as an attempt to deploy a global language to solve a local
problem; but in this choice of tactic matters of identity, context
or character can become lost in the process. 'It is impossible
to see what anyone means by "local character" any more
in London,' writes Fraser. Indeed, in Stratford, a couple of
miles to the northeast of the Shard, the site zoned off for
the Olympic Park has been subjected to a near-complete
transformation. Historic infrastructural elements inherited
from a century of industrialisation (canals, sewers) remain as
the skeleton on/within which 21st-century changes are being
grafted. The project represents such a rapid evolution of place
that it represents less a process of healing, scarring and bodily
renewal, and more one of careful amputation and replacement.
The Park appears to be a good example, therefore, of both
regeneration and generation – that is, (re)generation – in that it
encompasses a complex mix of renewing an urban inheritance
and conjuring new landscapes completely afresh.

Bounded by major roads, railways lines and waterways,
the danger with this large site is that it suggests a wholly
defensive character; described by the chasms of transport
infrastructure, it has obvious security assets in Games mode
that could become problematic after the Games, when
temporary sporting structures are swept away to make room
for housing and other community facilities. The island nature
of the site, easy to police and monitor, presents considerable
challenges to public officials whose job it is to coax any
regenerative benefits over the hard edges and into East London
generally. This is very much the ambition – to exploit the
magnitude of energy and investment in the actual development
site and use it as a catalyst for renewal across a wider sphere,
to the benefit of neighbours and zones beyond the urban
horizon. But, at present, it is hard to imagine. The railway line
that marks the eastern edge of the site offers a territorial edge
of such breadth and depth that the ground on either side of it
appears entirely unrelated – even estranged. Design teams are,
in fact, going to great lengths to try to ensure the site periphery
is more of a blur than an edge. Bridge building (both physical

and socially metaphorical) is ongoing, and the extensive parks and rejuvenated waterways that span the site (the so-called 'green lung') add a further connectivity that echoes the character of the pre-industrial Stratford. It is these edges, and the interior/exterior relationships they represent, described by Steven Tomlinson on pages 102–107, which should never be underestimated in (re)generation.

Regeneration, or its cousin near-erasure and replacement, struggles over the role of place. Traces often survive comprehensive development, through street patterns, names, the shape and size of plots or conditions of topography. Like the process of pentimento, in which hidden layers of paintings become visible as upper layers of paint slowly become translucent, certain characteristics or uses manage to push through. The physical environment can even resist change. The street pattern of medieval London, ravaged by fire in 1666, re-established itself (largely due to finance and questions of landownership) despite the efforts of Christopher Wren and John Evelyn to redraw the city along rational lines. In *London: From Punk to Blair*, Joe Kerr describes the way in which 'blow-downs', the demolition of residential tower blocks, became popular public events as local communities would gather to watch celebrities trigger controlled explosions, creating a spectacle of smoke and rubble. At one such event in 1986, Kerr remembers a 1960s block becoming enveloped in dense white dust:

> As that dispersed, all eyes strained to see the expected void where for a generation that ugly and unloved Goliath had stood as a blemish on the landscape. But we were in for a shock, for, as the air slowly cleared, a strange object loomed out of the mist where there should have been only sky visible. It quickly became apparent that the explosion had merely blown out the bottom four or five storeys of the tower, leaving a battered stump tottering at a precarious angle.[4]

The street pattern of medieval London, ravaged by fire in 1666, re-established itself (largely due to finance and questions of landownership) despite the efforts of Christopher Wren and John Evelyn to redraw the city along rational lines.

The South Bank, above Waterloo Bridge, 2011
top: A century of change. A similar view to that illustrated in HW Brewer's *A Half Century's Change* of 1899. The industrial south bank has become London's new centre for culture, a change that began with the 1951 Festival of Britain.

HW Brewer, *A Half Century's Change in London*, 1899
centre: Views south across the Thames, from a point near Waterloo Bridge, in 1848 and 1898.

Olympic Park blue fence
bottom left: The 17.7-kilometre (11-mile) boundary of the site of the Olympic Park was marked by a notorious blue fence, installed in September 2007. This example, on White Post Lane, was one of few remnants of the plywood structure by the summer of 2011.

Housing, Leyton Road, Stratford, London, 2011
bottom right: One of the tests of the regenerative nature of the London 2012 Olympic and Paralympic Games will be the extent to which they can improve the lives of people across the boundary of the development site, such as the occupants of these houses on Leyton Road.

VIEW FROM A POINT NEAR WATERLOO BRIDGE IN 1848   FROM A SKETCH MADE ON THE SPOT BY "W.D" JULY 1848.

VIEW FROM THE SAME POINT IN 1898.   BY MR H. W. BREWER.

A HALF-CENTURY'S CHANGE IN LONDON.

17.7

LENGTH OF FENCE AROUND THE OLYMPIC PARK SITE IN KILOMETRES

Blow-downs and other tools of demolition which scrape sites clean lie at the extreme end of (re)generation. Because of the all-or-nothing approach, the new intervention is always an import, based on practices or forces from elsewhere and applied to the cleared site with a certain degree of faith. Or an unsentimental hard-headedness – what Iain Sinclair calls 'a beat the clock impatience unrivalled in London since the beginnings of the railway age'.[5] Peter Bishop argues on pages 28–31 that regeneration is more convincing when it works with the found condition of the site, using social and physical characteristics to best advantage and giving communities or sites the best chance of retaining any sense of place. Further, he presents a compelling case for a loose-fit planning strategy, based not on definitive masterplans, but rather on a strong sense of direction and vision. This way, attempts at regeneration are a little unplanned, making room for things to happen without being entirely prescriptive. It is, instead of a statutory and immovable check list, a method for betterment based on broad aspirations, a sound understanding of place and community, and creating chances for the unexpected and unplannable.

A mechanism like this, a touch unconventional and perhaps not always appropriate, sits comfortably with the history of London with its curious mixture of the planned and the unplanned. It also leaves room for complexity and the notion that places are not merely architectural, but social, cultural, political, psychological, emotional and economic. There is always the danger that comprehensive development begats comprehensive development, in that a single overarching plan can too closely match the cultural values and conditions of a particular time, straitjacketing the needs of future generations (witness postwar Elephant and Castle or Edwardian White City). Regeneration implies a little scar tissue, because one can never quite tell how wounds are going to heal. The 1949 Ealing comedy *Passport to Pimlico* begins with a shopkeeper's vision to transform a bomb site into a smart new swimming pool; by the end of the film the community is happy with rain. ⌂

Christopher Wren, Plan for rebuilding the City of London after the Great Fire of 1666
Wren's vision of squares and grand avenues never materialised, and the city re-established itself along its medieval pattern.

Notes
1. I Turok, 'Property-Led Urban Regeneration: Panacea or Placebo?', *Environment and Planning A*, Vol 24, 1992, pp 36 1–79.
2. S Batty, 'The Gamble of Urban Regeneration', *Environment and Planning B*, Vol 30, 2003, p 486.
3. K Powell, *City Reborn: Architecture and Regeneration in London, from Bankside to Dulwich*, Merrell (London), 2004, p 10.
4. J Kerr and A Gibson, *London: From Punk to Blair*, Reaktion Books (London), 2003, 192–3.
5. I Sinclair, *Ghost Milk: Calling Time on the Grand Project*, Hamish Hamilton (London), 2011, p 57.

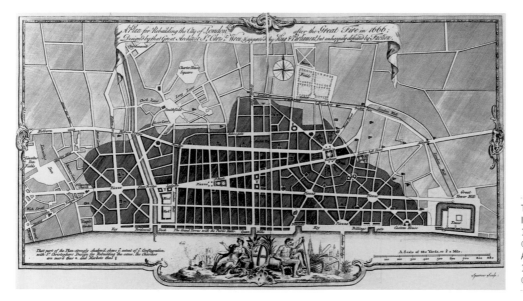

Murray Fraser

Peter Barber Architects, Goldhawk Road, Shepherd's Bush, London, due for completion 2014
The project relies on a high-density mixed-use composition with open pedestrian circulation to encourage street interaction.

London today has become 'a laboratory and testing ground' for neoliberal capitalism, attracting investment from the Middle East, Russia, India, the Far East and Australasia as well as the US. **Murray Fraser** describes the urban impact of economic globalisation in the capital, while exploring ways that it might potentially be countered.

THE GLO
ARCHITE
INFLUEN
ON LON

BAL
CTURAL
CES
DON

It is a constituent of urban regeneration that it involves new
processes of growth once cities recover from periods of economic
hiatus, man-made conflict or natural disaster. Not only do
regeneration projects literally consist of different collections
of atoms, they also infuse new approaches into whichever city
they are in. Today the change for London lies in switching from
previously dominant urban development models, stemming
largely from America, to a condition that is openly global and
multivalent. London is now part of a worldwide urban network
that is shooting different nerve reactions across its emergent
urban fabric. The prevailing mindset is that of neoliberal
capitalism turned into urban phenomena, prompting us to find
ways to counter this process. What, indeed, can be construed as
the positive aspects of globalisation? Doreen Massey writes of
the period after the 'Big Bang' of financial deregulation in the
City of London during the 1980s:

> London, or more precisely its financial constellation, was at
> the heart of the establishment of neoliberalism as hegemonic.
> Its fortunes were built on deregulation, privatisation and
> marketisation, and it was these forces that spread through the
> country and around the world.[1]

In other words, London is one of the places where economic
globalisation is being evolved as a concept and also being put
into practice – a laboratory and testing ground, as it were. This
in turn creates a greater number of external influences on its
architecture and urbanism, coming no longer just from the US,
but also from the Middle East, Russia, India, the Far East and
Australasia. It is part of London's ethnic/cultural mixity and
demotic cosmopolitanism that allows it to claim to be a 'world
city'. Or as Massey points out: 'Cities are central to neoliberal
globalisation. The increasing concentration of humanity within
them is in part a product of it.'[2]

Cross-cultural influences on city growth are nothing new;
indeed, Britain experienced the impact of American architecture
and urbanism, coupled with financial investment and cultural
sway, from the late 19th century.[3] Money, technology and design
ideas flowed into London, as in the Northern, Piccadilly and
other turn-of-the-century underground railway lines, or the
new offices and apartment blocks such as Bush House and
Ideal House, or the signature projects by Raymond Hood,
Eero Saarinen and so on. Following the Second World War,
the American influence became even stronger on London's
architecture and urbanism, reaching a high-tide mark in the
1980s with Thatcherite financial deregulation. From that arrived
major US commercial practices such as Skidmore, Owings &
Merrill (SOM), HOK and Swanke Hayden Connell, epitomised
by the new office cities of Broadgate and Canary Wharf. It
was fully noticed at the time, with Andrew Rabeneck noting
perceptively in the *Architects' Journal* in March 1990 (also
providing one of the earliest references to globalisation in British
architectural writing):

> This invasion of allies [from America] results partly from the
> local construction boom of the 1980s, but almost as much
> from the 'globalisation' of building design and construction,
> for which the oil-driven overseas boom of the 1970s was but
> a dress rehearsal.[4]

Interestingly, the impact of American ideas and practices
included aspects that are not usually regarded as US specialities,
such as historic building conservation and urban regeneration.
The outcome was the transference of urban niche marketing
to preserve the character of 'decaying' cities like London.
It had been the creation of the New York City Council's
Landmarks Preservation Committee in 1965, and the polemics
of US conservationists like Ada Louise Huxtable and Jane
Jacobs, which turned the tide in the battle to retain original
street patterns and high proportions of old buildings as vital
components in an economically diverse urban policy.[5] Market-
led redevelopment of historic buildings into exclusive urban
shopping destinations – known quaintly as 'place marketing'
– was imported to London at Covent Garden in the 1970s.
Pioneering the way was James Rouse, possibly the most
influential retail developer in postwar America; he had begun
with a private new town on British garden city principles at
Columbia, Maryland, but increasingly turned his attentions to
regenerating the downtown of nearby Baltimore.[6]

In Rouse's schemes in the run-down heart of Baltimore
from the mid-1960s, he devised two strategies that were applied
to other cities such as Boston, New York and San Francisco.

Renzo Piano Building Workshop (RPBW),
The Shard, London Bridge, due for
completion 2012
below: The new Shard tower shown in a
panoramic view of the river skyline.

bottom: Photomontage of the Shard
looming over the surrounding streetscape.

Golden Resources Mall, Beijing, late
2000s.
right: A brazen example of the new malls
being erected as part of China's rapid
economic expansion.

The first was the regeneration of dockside swathes into
prestigious waterfront business districts with showpiece
attractions – aquariums always loomed large – on the proviso
that 'enterprise zones' were established (as was later copied by
the London Docklands Development Corporation). Rouse's
second strategy was the remodelling of the finest historic
buildings into festival marketplaces to act as tourist magnets.
The refurbishment of the Ghirardelli chocolate factory
in San Francisco is seen as the prototype, but the concept
was pushed further by Rouse and his chosen architects,
Benjamin and Jane Thompson, when renovating Faneuil
Hall/Quincy Market in Boston (1971–6). That scheme was
an instant commercial and critical success, even if this meant
exaggerating its history as a brazenly themed food-court
environment. Thus when Covent Garden Market reopened in
London in 1980, one reviewer claimed the Greater London
Council (GLC) had 'produced an internationally important
example of urban conservation on a par with the Faneuil Hall
scheme in Boston'.[7] Later in the US were a host of highly
publicised urban regeneration schemes by Rouse's company
– mostly designed by Benjamin Thompson Associates – of
which the most visited was the Fulton Market/South Street
Seaport Museum in Manhattan.

The influence on London's regeneration projects from
the 1970s is undoubted, not only at Covent Garden, but also,
for example, in the refurbished St Katherine's Dock, next to
Tower Bridge, and elsewhere. Rouse searched for his own
urban regeneration projects in Britain, but nothing was on
the cards when he died in 1996. Plenty of other developers
and architects in London, however, spread the approach, and
today we can still see, for instance, that heritage conservation
forms the heart of the King's Cross regeneration plan. But
it is equally important to note that the tide is turning in
London due to approaches stemming from other parts of the
world not so tied to historic conservation, and it is significant
that several major redevelopment projects – typified by the
site of the London 2012 Olympic and Paralympic Games in
Stratford – are being promoted as defiant newbuild schemes
that seem to reject the existing urban fabric. It is worth
looking at some of these projects.

The influence on London's regeneration
projects from the 1970s is undoubted, not
only at Covent Garden, but also, for example,
in the refurbished St Katherine's Dock, next
to Tower Bridge, and elsewhere.

Delirious New London

Essential to the spread of global neoliberalist capitalism is wealth production, not of course by actually making things, but by redistributing capital and data flows and linking these to tourism. As the current director of Canary Wharf observes of London's position following the global economic recession that began in early 2008:

> The landscape is changing and London is growing. It went through a very bad credit crunch but, when you come out of it, London will still be the hub of the financial world. In a way, Canary Wharf was a precursor of what's happening in King's Cross, Paddington Basin and Battersea.[8]

He could have added London Bridge/Bermondsey as another district currently being regenerated on the business model grown in the 'Petri dish' of Canary Wharf. Today, near to the City of London and south of the river at a major transport interchange node, rises the Shard, London Bridge. The tower, designed by the celebrated Italian architect Renzo Piano, will be 310 metres (1,017 feet) high and thus soar over the UK's previous tallest structure, the 235-metre (771-foot) high Canary Wharf tower; indeed, the Shard is to be the tallest building in Europe (even if paltry compared to the 800-metre (2,625-foot) high Burj Khalifa in Dubai). Aesthetically, the Shard is fully glazed and anachronistic, making the observer unsure whether it is boldly futuristic or totally retro (probably the latter). The scheme hastens the gentrification of the Bermondsey and Elephant and Castle areas, and already protests are gathering about its effect on local communities and shopping clusters around its massive base.[9] It effectively pushes the corporate values of the City of London or Canary Wharf into South London for the very first time, creating what is being claimed as 'London's third business district'.

Along with the main tower, Piano has designed a smaller scheme, The Place, right next door for the same developer, Sellar Properties. This offers a new public square and bus terminal between the Shard and the refurbished London Bridge railway/underground station. James Sellar, son of the developer who conceived the proposal, says: 'In the London Bridge quarter we are trying to create a cosmopolitan area, which means getting the balance right between mixed-use buildings and local character.'[10] It is impossible to see what anyone means by 'local character' any more in London, but in terms of providing a high-density mixed-use building, the Shard cannot be interpreted as anything other than a global project. The Shard was only saved from failure in 2008 when a consortium of Qatari banks put in £150 million to buy an 80 per cent stake. The building's main secured tenant, and the anchor of its financial success, is the Hong Kong luxury chain Shangri-La Hotels, showing that it is global money driving the initiative. Nearby in Bermondsey will be a new branch of Jay Jopling's upmarket art gallery, White Cube, again part of the international art scene and nothing to do with the urban locality. Other art establishments like Shunt are being squeezed out as a result of this globalised gentrification process in London, which is precisely what alarms local residents.

Asian-Style Shopping

Spectacle is a major emphasis of the consumption-driven nexus of global neoliberalism, as David Harvey points out.[11] Again, globalised money is increasingly calling the shots in London, as seen, for example, in the donation by Lakshmi Mittal, Britain's wealthiest man, albeit an Indian steel magnate, of the ArcelorMittal Orbit public sculpture designed by Anish Kapoor as a symbol for the London 2012 Games. As part of the same regeneration initiative – widely criticised for erasing local community facilities – the largest urban shopping centre in Europe, Westfield Stratford City, is being completed at the staggering cost of £1.45 billion. It will act as the main gateway for the Games when they are on.[12] Opened in September 2011, the Westfield Stratford offers 190,000 square metres (2.04 million square feet) of retail space in 300 shops as well as offices, a hotel, casino and so on. Reportedly 8,500 jobs will be created as a result. Its shopping outlets are already almost fully taken. The key descriptor is that it is an 'urban' shopping centre, and thus a consciously different model to the American suburbanised mall which arrived in Britain in the 1970s at Brent Cross and reached its apogee at Bluewater in Kent.

Now that government policy on all political sides is against approving any more out-of-town regional shopping malls, there is clear pressure to adopt Asian high-density urban precedents. The Stratford project is being built by an Australian company,

90

THE MILLIONS OF GBP THE
US GOVERNMENT PAID FOR
THE 5-ACRE SITE FOR ITS
NEW EMBASSY

Westfield, but using an Asian urban mall typology as found in Tokyo, Singapore, Hong Kong, Beijing or Shanghai. It also represents a virtual mirror image of the already successful (although smaller) Westfield London mall that opened in 2008 in Shepherd's Bush in West London. Both have a relaxed Asian-style collagist aesthetic which combines fragments of recent architectural styles along with sections of open-air 'street', replete with alfresco eating opportunities, to convey a sense of urban hipness.

A noticeable divergence in Westfield Stratford City is the move away from the usual 'dumbell' layout based on large anchor stores; indeed, John Lewis is its only real department store, this being that company's first new store in London for 20 years. If anything, it is Westfield Stratford's other infrastructural elements – stadium, station and hotel – which act as the magnets to attract shoppers. Yet in other ways, Westfield Stratford uses the typical tricks of shopping centres, not least since an estimated 70 per cent of visitors to the 2012 Games, some 360,000 people on peak days, will need to pass through the mall on their way to and from events. In terms of its 'legacy' after the Games, the worry is that this urban megamall will suck trade away from surrounding shops in East London, in the manner that out-of-town malls have blighted regional towns for decades now.[13]

Westfield Stratford's catchment is the 4.1 million people in London, Kent and Essex who happen to live within a 45-minute drive from Stratford via the M11 link, plus those from its revived public transport links (underground trains, overground trains from St Pancras, Docklands Light Railway and possibly Crossrail if built). The project taps into the gentrification of East London as more artists, architects, designers and young professionals with relatively high disposable incomes buy homes or workspaces in these poorer areas. In that sense, the move by John Lewis, including one of its de luxe Waitrose supermarket stores, cannily anticipates the shift of wealth. Westfield Stratford will have a fresh food market, boutique shops and celebrity chef restaurants, including reputedly one run by Jamie Oliver. If only they could persuade Eurostar trains to stop off in Stratford, the developers would have it made.

Also tellingly, while many ordinary shops in the streets of London were left for hours as virtual free-for-alls during the mass riots of 8 August 2011, the Metropolitan Police – purportedly after picking up subversive chatter on social networking sites – moved rapidly to protect the Westfield malls in Shepherd's Bush and Stratford, along with the whole site of the Games.[14] In this way, social and economic tensions connected to such symbolic regeneration projects were suppressed.

Circle the Wagons!

Having created wealth via the neoliberal capitalist system, one needs, however, to defend it using all the political and military forces at one's disposal. South of London's river, in the traffic melting pot of Vauxhall, the massive regeneration of the area around Battersea Power Station is being shaped by another harsh global reality: America's defensiveness in the face of losing its economic and political power to the Far East. Now that the US Embassy in Grosvenor Square – completed in 1960 to Eero Saarinen's design, and still the only American embassy in the world not owned by the US (it is rented at a peppercorn rent from the Duke of Westminster's Grosvenor Estate) – is regarded as a security risk, it is distressingly surrounded by anti-terrorist barriers which disfigure a once-lovely square. For the anti-terrorist mentality that drives US power these days, the only solution is to quit the messy complexities of Grosvenor Square and find a more defendable place to hitch one's wagons. The 2-hectare (5-acre) site in Vauxhall was purchased by the US government for £90 million, with the new embassy due for occupation in 2017. A design competition was held, won by the Philadelphia-based practice of KieranTimberlake; its scheme is a bland glass cube set into its own traffic roundabout system and encircled by defensive measures disguised by greenery. This urban strategy is being overseen by a leading UK architect/ masterplanner, Terry Farrell, who states: 'The aim is to turn it to one's benefit by making a defensive area around the embassy take the form of landscape. It means everyone can look at landscape instead of looking at it like fortifications like at Grosvenor Square.'[15] The decision about the winning scheme was apparently taken by the US Ambassador to Britain, reflecting the political and military basis for the selection rather than architectural or urbanistic qualities. For instance, other designs submitted for the competition found a better reception, such as the dramatic entry by Morphosis, but they were not so eminently defendable. Under American anti-terrorist codes, every new US embassy

There are symptoms of a more appealing urban diversity being forged out of market-led globalising impulses.

needs a 35-metre (115-foot) exclusion zone around it. Even more worryingly, the masterplan surrounds the embassy with a so-called 'natural fortification' in the shape of Embassy Gardens, an exclusive 6-hectare (15-acre) scheme designed by Farrell for the Ballymore Group and consisting of an urban square, 2,000 homes, a 100-bedroom hotel, 50,000 square metres (538,195 square feet) of offices, and 13,000 square metres (139,930 square feet) of shops, bars and restaurants. Its highest housing block will rise up 23 storeys. The urban design aspect is being heavily talked up by Farrell, who says the combined project 'would rival the Thameside regeneration of east London'.[16] Why the paranoid defensive mindset of a beleaguered international power is the right way to plan a city is not discussed.

Alternative Possibilities

If the above projects, and others that could be cited, hint at a London regeneration system in disarray, that indeed seems the case. Neoliberalist capitalism thrives on crisis, and as such drives out more expansive or communally minded solutions. But this also means the need is to resist and find other exemplars, which is where many of London's best younger architects are operating. And there are symptoms of a more appealing urban diversity being forged out of market-led globalising impulses. For example, a new economy based on design, media and Web-based digital technology is emerging in Shoreditch, just north of the City of London. Here, small firms are taking advantage of cheaper rents, ultra-hip bars and galleries, coffee shops, restaurants, and an openly gritty inner-city location that is culturally distinct from the glamorous swank of London's West End or districts like Chelsea and Notting Hill. The area's busiest junction, the Old Street roundabout – recently given a makeover in an urban design scheme by Tonkin Liu, an architectural practice which worked in Hong Kong in the 1990s before moving to London – is now being called, tongue in cheek, 'Silicon Roundabout'.[17] The nickname reflects the presence of a number of internet and social networking firms in the area, such as TweetDeck, a spin-off from Twitter. The phenomenon represents what economists call 'milieu culture' whereby companies and people of the same age and interests overlap socially and economically, meeting in pubs and bars to swap information and find new jobs/new employees. It is an intriguing

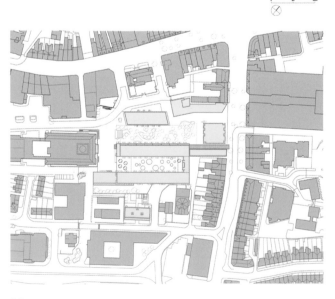

Peter Barber Architects, Proposal for Cromwell Square, North Kensington, London, 2009
right: A corner tower suggests an urban presence and lively views of the busy Cromwell Road for apartment residents.

if intangible strategy, linked to the idea of festivals and other events to launch 'East London Tech City'. Of course it does not offer all the answers, and indeed could be accused of self-consciously promoting the 'creative cities' claptrap of Richard Florida and others; such views are in fact merely the latest branded version of urban boosterism whereby capitalism uses city redevelopment as a means of surplus investment whenever commodity production is in downturn.[18]

More importantly in architectural and urbanistic terms for London are the cases where architects are seeking to divert the same urban regeneration forces into more interstitial and socially minded approaches. Perhaps obviously, many of the fruitful locations lie in the lesser known and somewhat forlorn areas of the capital. Out to the east, in Barking, the practice of Allford Hall Monaghan Morris (AHMM) has since 2004 been overseeing a bold revival of the town centre with new apartments, a library, art gallery, hotel, shops and restaurants, coupled with an urban square designed by muf architecture/art. To the western side of the city, in proposals such as for Goldhawk Road and Cromwell Square, Peter Barber Architects employs its signature Corbusier-meets-the-Casbah model of high-density mixed-use urbanism to create nodes for a revitalised city. Barber's designs are based openly on the ways people socialise in streets, as observed by Walter Benjamin in the 1920s and later philosophised in Hannah Arendt's concept of the 'space of appearance'.[19] It is such examples that offer a vision which is more vibrant, and indeed more socially and ecologically sustainable, than the old-fashioned office towers, malls and embassies that will only diminish London as a cosmopolitan entity. ∆

Notes
1. Doreen Massey, *World City*, Polity Press (Cambridge/Malden, MA), 2010, p x.
2. Ibid, p 9.
3. Murray Fraser with Joe Kerr, *Architecture and the 'Special Relationship': The American Influence on Post-War British Architecture*, Routledge (London/New York), 2007.
4. Andrew Rabeneck, 'The American Invasion', *Architects' Journal*, Vol 191, No 13, 28 March 1990, p 38.
5. AL Huxtable, 'Preservation in New York', *Architectural Review*, August 1962, pp 83–5; Jane Jacobs, *The Death and Life of Great American Cities*, Random/Cape (New York/London), 1961/94, pp 200–12: Robert Stern et al, *New York 1960: Architecture and Urbanism Between the Second World War and the Bicentennial*, Monacelli Press (New York), 1995, pp 1091–153, 1210–11.
6. Colin Amery, Mark Girouard and Dan Cruickshank, 'Save the Garden', *Architectural Review*, July 1972, pp 16–32; S Cantacuzino, *New Uses for Old Buildings*, Architectural Press (London), 1975; David Gosling with MC Gosling, *The Evolution of American Urban Design*, Wiley-Academy (Chichester), pp 84–7; Joshua Olsen, *Better Places, Better Lives: A Biography of James Rouse*, Urban Land Institute (Washington DC), 2003, pp 269–70.
7. 'A London Masterpiece Restored', *Architectural Review*, September 1980, p 138.
8. George Iacobescu, Director of Canary Wharf plc, quoted in Oliver Shah, 'Canary Wharf developer on a fishing trip up the Thames', *Sunday Times*, 29 May 2011, 'Business', p 6.
9. Jonathan Glancey, 'Shard to Become Europe's Tallest Building', *Guardian*, 24 November 2010, p 8; Kieran Long, 'The Shard Effect', *Evening Standard*, 5 May 2011, pp 24–5.
10. Kieran Long, op cit, p 24.
11. David Harvey, *The Conditions of Postmodernity: An Enquiry Into the Origin of Cultural Change*, Basil Blackwell (Oxford/Cambridge, MA), 1989.
12. The analysis here is largely taken from: Nicholas Jewell, 'Socialism and Shopping', PhD thesis, Bartlett School of Architecture, University College London, currently in progress; Nicholas Jewell, 'The Fall and Rise of the British Shopping Mall', *The Journal of Architecture*, Vol 6, No 4, Winter 2001, pp 317–78.
13. Rebecca Smithers, 'Europe's Largest Shopping Centre', *Guardian* 'Money', 21 May 2011, pp 1–2; Jonathan Prynn, 'Top Retailers Rush to Claim a Space in Stratford Mall', *Evening Standard*, 14 July 2011, p 18.
14. 'Riots Thwarted by Blackberry and Twitter Chat – Police', BBC News website, 16 August 2011, www.bbc.co.uk/news/uk-politics-14542588, accessed 18 August 2011.
15. Mark Blunden, 'New US Embassy to Use Landscape as "Fortifications"', *Evening Standard,* 5 May 2011, p 4.
16. Ibid.
17. Josh Halliday, 'Britain's Web Entrepreneurs Chase Traffic at Silicon Roundabout', *Guardian*, 28 May 2011, p 30.
18. Richard Florida, *The Rise of the Creative Class: And How It's Transforming Work, Leisure, Community and Everyday Life*, Basic Books (New York), 2002.
19. Walter Benjamin, 'One Way Street ' [1928], in *One Way Street and Other Writings*, Verso (London), 1997; Hannah Arendt, *The Human Condition*, University of Chicago Press (Chicago, IL), 1958/98; George Baird, *The Space of Appearance*, MIT Press (Cambridge, MA), 1995; M Fraser, 'Beyond Koolhaas', in Jane Rendell et al (eds), *Critical Architecture*, Routledge (London/New York), 2007, pp 332–9.

Edward Denison

LONDON THE SHAR

Renzo Piano Building Workshop (RPBW), The Shard,
London Bridge, London, due for completion 2012
Artist's impression of the Shard viewed from the southwest.

BRIDGE/
D

London Bridge is no stranger to revolution. It was here in 1381 that Wat Tyler and his Kentish mob crossed the Thames during the Peasants' Revolt and some days later his severed head was impaled on a pike. Today, another spike is marking a different kind of revolution at London Bridge. Rising above London Bridge railway station on the site of the forgettable Southwark Tower, the Shard, designed by Renzo Piano for the Sellar Property Group, is a 310-metre (1,017-foot) high acicular tower that will be western Europe's tallest building. It is the conspicuous centrepiece in the high-profile regeneration of the station and the surrounding historic district of London Bridge, which marketeers are busily rebranding London Bridge Quarter (LBQ).

Regeneration, more than mere development, consciously embraces history and at London Bridge the layers of history run particularly deep, enriching one of London's most ambitious regeneration projects. Until the 1990s, London Bridge was the City's piteous neighbour, but with the improvement of the nearby docklands and the establishment of regeneration agencies such as the Pool of London Partnership in 1996, things started to change. The arrival of the Jubilee Line extension in time for the millennium celebrations and the placement of the newly founded City Hall nearby were two major milestones towards the area's improvement, but the biggest changes (quite literally) are taking place throughout this decade and will transform London for decades to come.

The first phase is the Shard, a mixed-use building containing offices for approximately 12,000 workers, 'world-renowned' restaurants, a 205-room five-star hotel, 5,760 square metres (62,000 square feet) of exclusive residential space, and a public observation deck. The entire project narrowly escaped being scuppered in 2007, before the intervention of a Qatari sovereign investment fund; 80 per cent of LBQ is now Qatari owned. Towering over London's ancient skyline, the 72-storey Shard has reignited the long-running debate about building heights and sightlines that began in the late 19th century with the 50-metre (164-foot) high Queen Anne's Mansions near St James's Park. The legislation that this fabled Babylonian building triggered restricted building heights in London and prevented the capital's lofty aspirations at a time when the skyscraper was taking off elsewhere in the world.

Over a century later, despite London's more permissive attitude compared with many of its European counterparts, the debate continues to rage. While the Shard's supporters point to the building's vitality and its potential to stimulate change, and its detractors see it as another step in the inexorable march of ego-architecture, the Shard, whose construction alone is expected to cost around £425 million, has become the showpiece of a multibillion-pound regeneration scheme.

The Shard will be completed in time for the London 2012 Olympic and Paralympic Games, but the longer term improvements will not be completed until 2018. These include

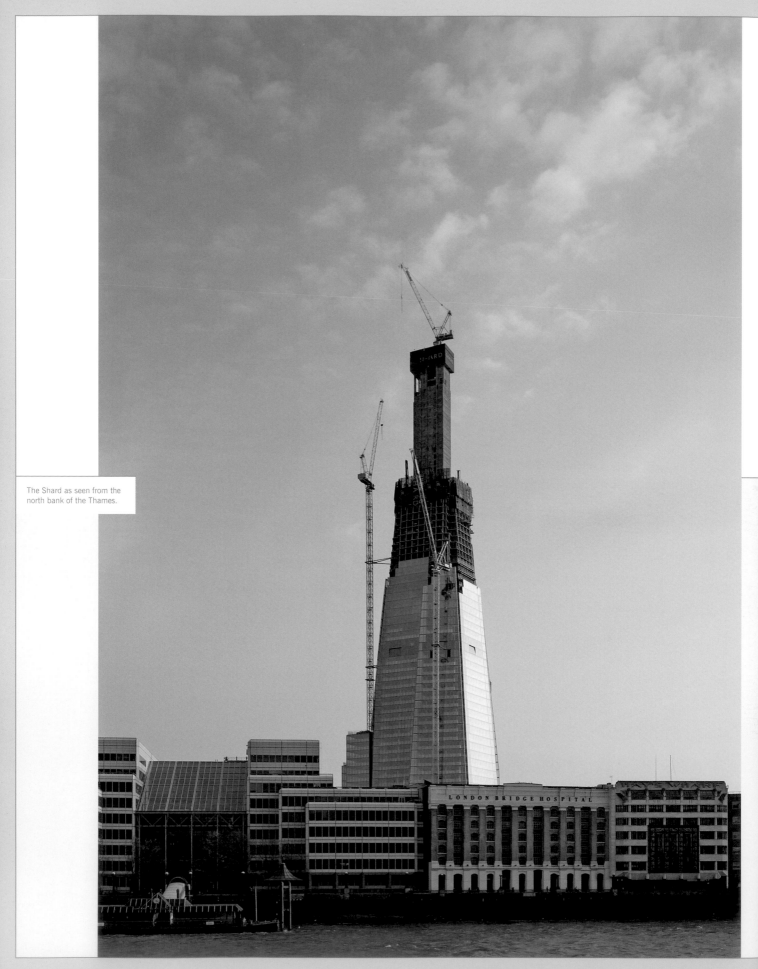

The Shard as seen from the north bank of the Thames.

the neighbouring 40,000-square-metre (430,556-square-foot) 17-storey office development, The Place (also designed by Piano), due to open in early 2013, and the complete regeneration of London Bridge railway station, which will start in the same year, transforming the experiences of the 54 million people who pass through it annually.

At the heart of the station's redevelopment is Network Rail's ambitious £6 billion plan to improve Thameslink, the capital's only north–south mainline railway service connecting Bedfordshire to the south coast via Central London. A new station concourse at street level on both Tooley and St Thomas streets will accommodate two-thirds more passengers and will help to better integrate the station with the surrounding environment including a new bus station. It will also provide more through-platforms to accommodate a larger number of longer Thameslink trains passing through the station, giving London Bridge frequent and seamless mainline connections with other regenerated transport hubs, including Crossrail at Farringdon and Eurostar at St Pancras. A revolution is under way at London Bridge, but to witness it one has to look beyond the Shard. △

54

THE MILLIONS OF PEOPLE
WHO PASS THROUGH
LONDON BRIDGE RAILWAY
STATION
EACH YEAR

top: Artist's impression of the Shard viewed from the northwest.

centre: Artist's impression of the proposed Tooley Street entrance to the new London Bridge station.

bottom: Artist's impression of the aerial view of London Bridge station's proposed Tooley Street entrance showing the Shard in the background.

Peter Bishop

Successful cities are constantly in the process of regeneration. The alternative is stasis and decline or being relegated to the margin of the heritage industry. Areas improve, decline or are redeveloped by the action of governments, private individuals or corporations. Sometimes described as 'gentrification' this change is normal and healthy. We cannot freeze our neighbourhoods or communities according to the fleeting prevailing circumstances of the present.

Emerging Practice in Regeneration

Defined good practice in regeneration has been arrived at through a long process of trial and error, and in response to an increasingly sophisticated understanding of the processes that need to be considered in long-term planning. The present period of urban planning and development is a watershed. It is possibly as significant as the end of the 19th century when the growth of democratic city government ushered in a century of urban planning based on an active public sector with sufficient power and resources at its disposal to physically shape cities. The fragmentation of political consensus, loss of faith in 'big government' and, in the Western economies at least, the economic downturn affecting business confidence and public expenditure, amount to an almost 'perfect storm' in relation to the usefulness of traditional planning strategies.

Alongside this, the ways of regenerating our cities are changing. The watershed was probably the City Challenge programmes introduced in the early 1990s by the then deputy prime minister Michael Heseltine. This programme brought forward two significant changes in practice. The first was

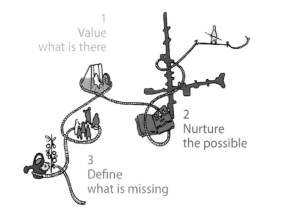

1
Value
what is there

2
Nurture
the possible

3
Define
what is missing

APPROACHES TO REGENERATION

Planning in the capital is at a watershed. Development has become almost entirely market-driven and the government's localism agenda now requires that local authorities take a back seat. Does this leave a role for inclusive regeneration strategies led by the public sector? **Peter Bishop** thinks so. He illustrates his argument with the work of Design for London and the London Borough of Newham at the Royal Docks in East London.

muf, Regenerating Dalston, Dalston, London, 2008
muf's work in Dalston for Design for London is based on a sophisticated understanding of the area's complexity. Their work articulated the wishes of the local community and translated these into a detailed regeneration programme.

that money would be allocated not according to need, based on indices of deprivation, but on competitive bidding. The second was that one of the principal criteria for success in this competition for funds would be the strength of the partnership, especially the involvement of the private sector, and new funding sources. In other words, the local authority's role was moved from provider to enabler.

This change in emphasis is now moving to a next stage. Under the current government's localism agenda, the proposition is that power shifts towards local residential neighbourhoods and business groups. The local authority might facilitate activity, but it will no longer be the initiator. This might, in some areas, unlock real energy for change, driven from the grass roots, but will it be sufficient to tackle some of the really difficult problems embedded in urban and rural areas? The market, in addition, is selective where it invests. Even in the boom period of 1996 to 2008 there were areas that were left behind to decline. In the post-2008 recession period, this appears likely to continue, and in some places indefinitely.

In London, much of the activity of regeneration is naturally market-driven. Most people would consider Covent Garden, Shoreditch and the South Bank as being successes. Canary Wharf, though not without its critics, has fundamentally changed not just a disused area of outmoded docks, but arguably has enabled London to continue to compete on global financial markets. We will have to wait to judge the affects of the London 2012 Olympic and Paralympic Games, but the work to tackle the contamination and dereliction of the Lea Valley is already of significance.

What is Regeneration?

'Regeneration' as a word, however, is becoming devalued to the point that it is losing any significant meaning. It used to justify action, whether civic, corporate or community. Like 'sustainability', it is used to imply something that is assumed by its very nature to be a good thing – after all, who would want to degenerate an area? It is used without thinking.

To be meaningful, regeneration needs to be a process to change a place, for the better, which is then capable of self-sustainment. It is a dynamic concept rather than an end state. It should therefore go beyond the physical and embrace the social and economic. This beneficial effect need not be general, but if specific to a selective group in society this should be explicit.

Regeneration may be triggered by either direct action, or the indirect nurturing of a set of circumstances that might cause positive change to happen. Either way, any process causing or leading to 'regeneration' has to involve a degree of value judgement. Regeneration cannot be a technical act. Its benefits are rarely universally or evenly spread. It therefore needs to be viewed in its political context.

An important element of successful regeneration process is that the planning vision should make use of the existing social and physical characteristics of an area, rather than eliminate them. Many practitioners now agree that urban projects should begin with a survey of all existing elements, planned or not, and that the individual qualities of a place should be enhanced by sculpting new programmes and places out of what is already there. This is shown very clearly by the work of architects muf in Dalston, where a comprehensive survey of the area developed

To be meaningful, regeneration needs to be a process to change a place, for the better, which is then capable of self-sustainment. It is a dynamic concept rather than an end state. It should therefore go beyond the physical and embrace the social and economic.

Village Underground, Shoreditch, London, 2007
Shoreditch has emerged in the last 10 years as one of London's most dynamic creative hubs. Village Underground combines studio, gallery and workspace within recycled tube trains on a previously unused viaduct site.

into a sophisticated regeneration programme that 'valued what is there, nurtured the possible and defined what is missing'. In a similar way, the case study of Bankside by Witherford Watson Mann (see pages 44–9) illustrates the way in which a long-term vision, based firmly on an appreciation of the characteristics and potential of the existing urban form, can be implemented flexibly, as and when the resources are available.

Inclusive Strategies

Any regeneration strategy should seek, through extensive processes of stakeholder engagement, to reach a wider consensus about the end product. But even the most ardent advocates of such community involvement would admit that the process is often difficult. A key adage of community engagement is that you can only ever engage people around their concerns. Large-scale long-term planning, by its very nature, finds it difficult to engage the concerns of the majority of people who focus on issues that happen in their immediate neighbourhood, or affect their daily lives or interests directly. The masterplan is often too remote, in terms of both time and scale, to reflect such concerns. There is greater scope to engage local stakeholders in interim planning, and from there to engage their interest in longer term scenarios. Interim-use 'charrettes' can help to demonstrate to stakeholders that there can be a transitional stage between what exists on a site now, and what might evolve as a semi-permanent state some time in the future. Importantly they can also demonstrate that this transitional or phased process offers a role for a far wider group of stakeholders than might normally be involved. It is the neighbouring communities who are most likely to understand the fine-grained dynamics and existing characteristics of a locality and the type of uses that might be grown to colonise an area.

So within this new environment, is there still a role for regeneration strategies led by the public sector? One of the

criteria for public-sector involvement concerns the need to address market imperfections. In Britain today there are no end of these, from ageing and overstretched infrastructure to inadequate housing and contaminated brownfield land. It is not just these areas, however – there are many others that are operating below their real economic potential, especially in town centres, or that are simply not pleasant places in which to live or work.

Case Study: The Royal Docks

The key to developing strategies is to understand fully the reasons why an area is declining or underperforming, and to fashion strategies that precisely address the factors contributing to failure. One example of this approach is illustrated by the work of Design for London and the London Borough of Newham in addressing the reasons why the Royal Docks in East London had not hitherto been regenerated successfully despite the proximity to the Central London economy and the previous investment in key projects such as transport infrastructure (the Jubilee Line and Docklands Light Railway), a university (the University of East London), an airport (London City) and a major music venue (the O2).

The 2008 property recession forced a rethink of previous strategy. The response was to abandon any attempt at masterplanning (there had been 73 masterplans and strategies for the area over the past 30 years) and consider looser strategic frameworks instead. The principal initiative was the Green Enterprise District (GED) which addressed three pressing imperatives. The first was London's need to diversify from its overdependence on financial services. The second was the mayor's desire for a single big idea on climate change, and the third was the need to brand and market an area where development activity had been very weak.

The GED brought these together into a very simple,

The key to developing strategies is to understand fully the reasons why an area is declining or underperforming, and to fashion strategies that precisely address the factors contributing to failure

Design for London, Royal Docks, East London, 2008–
This area had seen over 70 plans in the last 30 years. The solution for regeneration was to sweep these away and produce a looser strategy that defined the area's role in the London economy and that had cross-party political support.

overarching strategic framework. It proposed the allocation of land for research, technology, manufacturing and high-end recycling, and targeted companies within what was deliberately loosely defined as the 'green economy'. This was to be underpinned by investment in public infrastructure including district heating and energy networks, funded in association with the European Investment Bank via a £100 million revolving 'green' investment fund. A planning policy framework established high design and environmental specifications for all new development, and the London Development Agency (LDA) backed this up with residential and industrial retrofit programmes to improve energy performance. The final element was a proposition to seek a tourist/exhibition centre to showcase climate change and environmental issues.

This was never intended to be a plan; it was an aspiration and a branding exercise and was produced by Design for London in a matter of days. Sitting outside any legal or statutory framework, it was launched via the internet, conferences and exhibitions, including the 2010 Shanghai Expo. Word of mouth did the rest, resulting, for example, in Siemens deciding to locate its London research centre and environmental exhibition centre (due to open in July 2012) in the Royal Docks.

The next stage in the process was for Design for London to broker an alliance between the (Conservative) Mayor of London and the (Labour) mayor of the local borough, Newham. The alliance was significant in creating market confidence and was captured in a jointly signed 'vision' document, which was also non-statutory. The vision document swept away all previous masterplans and set out a simple joint objective to develop the Royal Docks as a business, hotel, conferencing, research and logistics district to support the Central London economy. In doing this it built on the area's strengths – its international airport, the O2 music venue and the ExCel Conference Centre. These are now being linked (across the Thames) by a cable car

funded by the mayor.

The final element of the strategy centred on land development. The mayor has substantial landholdings in the Royal Docks, and the next move was to incorporate a temporary-uses element into the process. Early in 2010 the magazine *Property Week* launched the 'Site Life' initiative to promote temporary uses as a means of rejuvenating large urban sites left empty by the property recession. In 'Meanwhile London', *Property Week* teamed up with the LDA and Newham borough to promote three sites as part of a longer term regeneration strategy on the back of the London 2012 Olympic and Paralympic Games.

Conclusions

It is, of course, arguable that the Royal Docks is a special case. This is undeniable, but then all regeneration work is around special cases. It is by its very nature bespoke. The principles, however, are more widely applicable: the idea of using simple but powerful concepts to get community and stakeholder engagement, the idea that planning strategies are loose, flexible and capable of adaptation to take advantage of events, and essentially a focus on process. Process is fundamental. With loose strategy it is possible to frame programmes consisting of lots of immediate small-scale actions that allow the local community to colonise their own area and enjoy the self-sustaining effects of their early successes.

But finally there is the intangible. In a world of financial spreadsheets, 'metrics', outputs, procurement 'professionals' and compliance, it is easy to lose sight of the very purpose behind urban generation. The purpose should be clear – to create better places for people to live in, work in and enjoy. In so doing, it is also necessary not lose sight of far more important 'outcomes' such as delight, chance, experimentation, risk, beauty and fun. ⌂

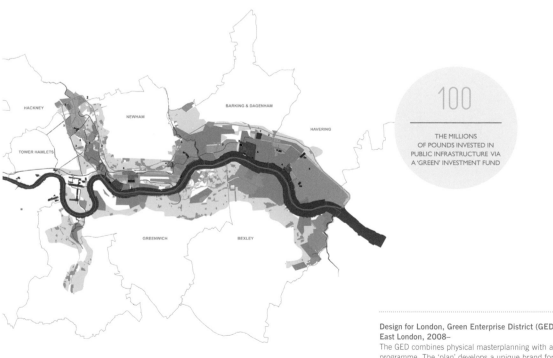

100

THE MILLIONS
OF POUNDS INVESTED IN
PUBLIC INFRASTRUCTURE VIA
A 'GREEN' INVESTMENT FUND

Design for London, Green Enterprise District (GED), Royal Docks, East London, 2008–
The GED combines physical masterplanning with an environmental programme. The 'plan' develops a unique brand for the area that is then articulated through more detailed area-based architectural design strategies.

John McAslan + Partners, Extension to King's Cross Station,
London, due for completion 2012
The project adds a new concourse to the west of the station,
which dates from 1852, as well as restoring the original facade.

KING'S

CROSS

100

ACRES THAT COMPRISE THE
WIDER DEVELOPMENT SITE
AT KING'S CROSS AND ST
PANCRAS

Twenty-seven hectares (67 acres) in extent, the King's Cross project is the largest renewal scheme in Central London; including the construction projects at King's Cross and St Pancras railway stations, the wider development site reaches to 40 hectares (100 acres). Roughly triangular in shape, the regeneration site sits between the two stations and fans out northwards, sited between railway lines and bisected by the Regent's Canal. When the project eventually completes around 2020, it will close the gap between the metropolitan bustle of the Euston Road and the residential zone of Camden to the north, long separated by railway yards and redundant gas works.

The scheme has been a long time coming; there was a period of six or seven years of detailed planning and consultation before even outline planning consent was granted by the London Borough of Camden. In fact, unusually, the borough (with the support of English Heritage) even granted 'enhanced outline consent' in 2007 rather than the detailed permission that would normally follow the earlier general approval. 'As long as we had detail enough to understand and assess likely impacts upon the historic environment we were happy to give the developer greater flexibility to respond to a changing market,' says an English Heritage statement.

The project can loosely be described as an office-led, mixed-use, high-density, medium-height development,

Bell Phillips + Kimble, Gas Holder No 8, King's Cross, London, 2009
above: One of a number of Victorian gas holders on the site, this structure is planned to be reinvented as an amphitheatre for public events and a water garden.

Stanton Williams, University of the Arts London, Central Saint Martins, King's Cross, London, 2011
below: A mid-19th-century granary building is converted into an art and design college; here an east–west link joins the Grade II listed building with a new extension.

comprising 743,224 square metres (8 million square feet) of new or refurbished buildings, of which 315,870 square metres (3.4 million square feet) will be commercial office space. There is also provision for 46,451 square metres (0.5 million square feet) of retail space and around 2,000 homes plus a 27-storey tower of student accommodation comprising 657 units. The student population is, in fact, an important element of the wider project; Central Saint Martins College of Art and Design (part of the University of the Arts London) moved on to the site in September 2011, occupying an extended Grade II listed granary building. Indeed, 92,903 square metres (1 million square feet) of the development is to be found within historic buildings and structures, including a housing development designed by Wilkinson Eyre that sits within the cast-iron framework of a trio of Victorian gas holders. Unfortunately this structure has been moved from its original location, along with gas holder number 8, which is to be developed as the frame for an outdoor leisure and swimming space.

Owned by King's Cross Central Limited Partnership, the project is being undertaken by Argent and a pair of masterplanners – Allies & Morrison and Porphyrios Associates, with landscaping by Townshend Landscape Architects. As is becoming typical with projects on such a large scale (Stratford, Elephant and Castle), Argent is working with multiple architects to create a certain diversity and an impression of organic growth from the beginning. Apart from those mentioned above, the scheme involves contributions from, among others, Glenn Howells, Stanton Williams, PRP, Niall McLaughlin and Bell Phillips.

In addition to the 50 buildings and 20 new streets under development within the project zone itself, a range of significant projects is taking place around the periphery of the site, including the recent completion of St Pancras Chambers (the Gothic frontage to the railway station), the extension and refurbishment of King's Cross station by John McAslan + Partners, and the creation of a new biomedical research centre called the Francis Crick Institute.

This wider programme of change and investment will no doubt shift the balance of property power in London. The east–west Euston Road was built as a bypass in 1756, and this large thoroughfare has generally acted as a barrier between the wealthier Georgian estates to the south and the poorer communities to the north. With its impressive transport connection, including the Eurostar, this new district marks the biggest change to the northern edge of the Euston Road since the advent of the railways. ∆

Townshend Landscape Architects, Pancras Square, King's Cross, London, due for completion 2014
below left: This new public square will provide a new north–south route for pedestrians, linking King's Cross station with the Regent's Canal and further development beyond.

Wilkinson Eyre Architects, Gas Holder Triplet Housing, King's Cross, London, ongoing
below right: Three gas holders are imaginatively reused as a container for 144 apartments. The Victorian structure has been dismantled for restoration and will be reassembled elsewhere within the development site.

King's Cross Central Limited Partnership, King's Cross development site, London, 2011
bottom left: The King's Cross development site in 2011. One gas holder structure is visible in the centre of the site, prior to dismantling for renovation. The King's Cross station and granary project (top right of the gas holder) are well under way.

King's Cross Central Limited Partnership, View of the completed King's Cross development, London, due for completion 2020
bottom right: This computer-generated visualisation illustrates the island nature of the site, sandwiched between two major railway stations and associated tracks.

Matthew Carmona

THE POLITICS OF LONDON'S STRATEGIC DESIGN

LON

Matthew Carmona tracks the vicissitudes of London's political engagement in urban design over the last decade. He reveals the strengths, weaknesses and remarkable similarities of the approaches of the two Mayors of London, Ken Livingstone and Boris Johnson

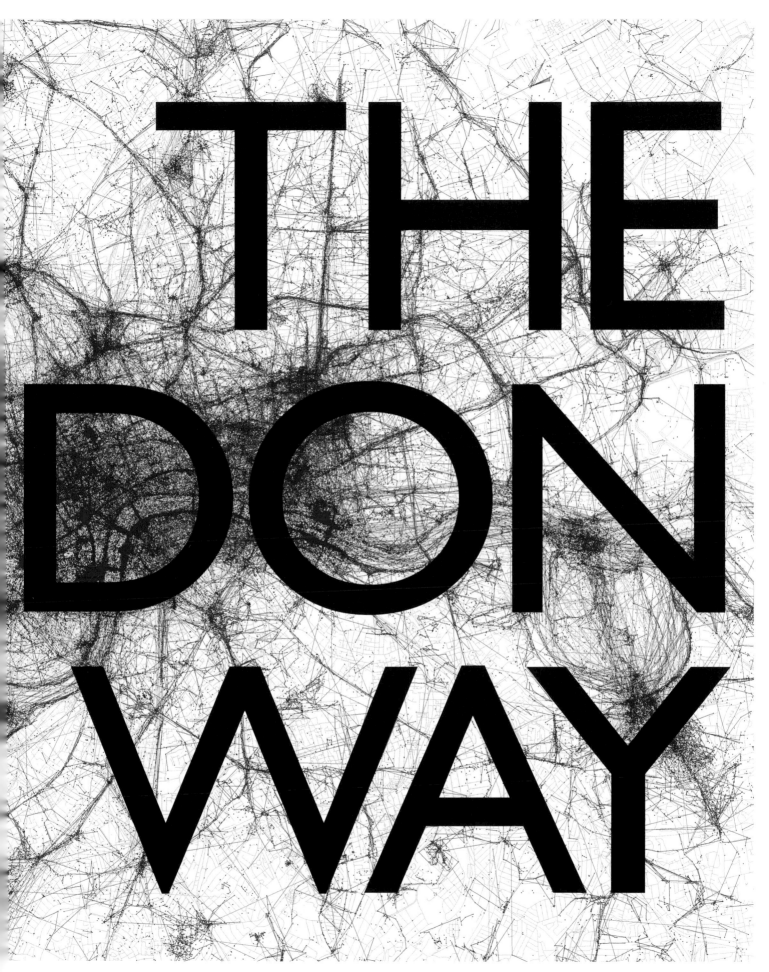

If its pre-1945 history, and the period from 1980 to 1997, demonstrated the typical processes of development in London, namely, let the market decide, then in political parlance this equates to the capitalist 'first way'. Similarly, the postwar period saw an attempt at an alternative, 'second way', just as it did in the national politics of the era, with the state taking on a much stronger leadership role, although constrained in what could be achieved by available resources and established land interests. Below is an exploration of how the intermediate, 'third way' characterised the development of London from 1997 to 2011, again reflecting wider trends in the national political scene. During this time the state tried to direct, once again, a stronger vision for the city, although implementation would largely be through market mechanisms with all the challenges and compromises, but also the resources and innovation, that implied.

A CITY OF CHANGE

The period since 2000 and the election of London's first city-wide mayor has seen a reinvigorated London-wide governance with an increasingly strong counterbalance at the strategic scale to the boroughs at the local level; although the latter retained most of the powers to actually deliver local services (including local planning). The first two London mayors have nevertheless shown that the position also encompasses a role as the capital's voice, providing a stage from which to speak out and be heard on all issues affecting it, whether or not actually covered by direct powers. One such issue is design.

The First Mayor

The national election of the Labour Party in 1997, followed by Ken Livingstone, with his reputation for radical left-wing

politics, as the first London mayor, might on the face of it have portended a return to a less favourable market environment. However, those who looked forward to the state once again expanding its role to become leader of development were quickly to be disappointed.

Although the role of the state did grow, for example the instigation of a new spatial planning system from 2004, the New Labour government of Tony Blair adopted (or more correctly continued) the neoliberal approaches of their predecessors, emphasising the vital importance of the market in economic and social policy, and of the state in enabling rather than directing development. To the surprise of many, Livingstone (who had fallen out with Labour and who in 2000 stood as an independent candidate) fully adopted the precepts of neoliberalism, although with a clear social justice tinge. From the start he signalled his intention to work closely with the business sector and the City of London Corporation, and to pursue an agenda for London based on growth. This was simply a pragmatic recognition that to achieve anything, Livingstone needed to work within the prevailing orthodoxy. But it was also a tacit acceptance that in the absence of direct public-sector investment, it was only through growth that many 'public goods' could be provided, including better public space. It was the 'third way' in action, although Livingstone himself would never have described it as such.

Although the London Plan that followed in 2004 addressed both this growth agenda and, to some commentators, a seemingly contrasting environmental one, it was not the wider environmental debates that tempered the drive for growth, but instead the design-led urban renaissance ideas of the mayor's adviser on architecture and urbanism, Richard Rogers. Thus the focus of the first London Plan was clearly on Central London,

Trafalgar Square
Today, Trafalgar Square offers a space reclaimed as the new centre of London life.

THE FIRST TWO LONDON MAYORS HAVE NEVERTHELESS SHOWN THAT THE POSITION ALSO ENCOMPASSES A ROLE AS THE CAPITAL'S VOICE, PROVIDING A STAGE FROM WHICH TO SPEAK OUT AND BE HEARD ON ALL ISSUES AFFECTING IT, WHETHER OR NOT ACTUALLY COVERED BY DIRECT POWERS. ONE SUCH ISSUE IS DESIGN.

and on the provision of higher-density mixed-use development, bringing people back into the city, and emphasising the importance of high-quality design. As such, although the Greater London Authority (GLA), which the mayor headed, was a strategic authority, he quickly found himself getting involved in what might have been considered by others to be local design matters.

100 Public Spaces

These ideas were reflected in Livingstone's most high-profile design-related initiative – the 100 Public Spaces programme. This the mayor launched with a fanfare in 2002, arguing that the quality of public space has a direct impact on the city's beauty, sustainability, prosperity, connectivity and safety; and promising to create or upgrade 100 public spaces over just five years. In fact, given the general lack of dedicated resources, the absence of any statutory role in this area, and lack of responsibility for the vast majority of public space in London (beyond the trunk road network), the early ambition proved rash, leading to a sense of failure when only five schemes had been realised five years later. Instead, huge landownership, development, funding and planning complexities quickly came to bedevil many of the schemes, with funding proving particularly problematic unless schemes could be cross-funded by large-scale development. The initiative firmly demonstrated the limitations of strategic and political will when reliant on the local boroughs and private actors to deliver.

This contrasted strongly with an early success scored by the mayor in one of just two spaces across the city for which he did have direct ownership and management responsibilities: the regeneration of Trafalgar Square. Although the vision (and

much of the technical work) to transform the space predated his mayoralty, Livingstone saw the project as a ready-made early win. The square has since moved from a neglected traffic-dominated urban fragment to the very essence of a renaissance space, becoming in the process a hugely popular and successful destination for Londoners. Yet its delivery by the public sector alone represented a departure from the predominant model of the time, one that more often than not relied on the private sector to take the lead.

Design Policy and Control

If the relative failure of the 100 Public Spaces programme showed the limitations of mayoral power, then the operation of his more prosaic strategic development control functions was potentially more far-reaching in its significance. The impact of these powers was certainly extremely tangible in sanctioning the renaissance-inspired drive towards an intensified central city (often in the face of opposition from the boroughs). It was also tangible in supporting the delivery of higher urban design standards in relation to many major developments, such as those planned for the Isle of Dogs where strategic development control powers were wielded to great effect to encourage a stronger focus on the public realm. Yet elsewhere the mayor's presence was hardly felt, for example at King's Cross Railway Lands 27.1 hectares (67 acres of prime redevelopment opportunity in Central London) where a competent team at the London Borough of Camden made strategic intervention unnecessary.

The experience of strategic development control (and Trafalgar Square) revealed an important demand on the mayor, namely the need to prioritise, and only to intervene where the impact might be maximised and/or the results reflected in

Café culture
Café culture spread across London in the 1990s and 2000s, as here at Festival Riverside.

2002 YEAR THE 100 PUBLIC SPACES PROGRAMME WAS LAUNCHED

practice elsewhere. This the mayor did successfully (alongside national policy), to spread his urban renaissance agenda beyond the GLA to the local boroughs and to development interests in London. His small but influential Architecture and Urbanism Unit (later, Design for London), for example, quickly learned to work in partnership with other organisations within the GLA family, with the boroughs, and with private interests to produce a range of design strategies across London (mainly in the Thames Gateway, east of London) that together represent admirable attempts to inject some physical vision back into London planning, although (as yet) with limited impact on the ground. For Londoners, this was undeniably a period when a noticeable new embrace of public space was apparent (perhaps for the first time since the Victorians' parks movement) as café culture came to the capital.

A CITY OF RETRENCHMENT

In May 2008, the charismatic, but somewhat unpredictable figure of Boris Johnson replaced Ken Livingstone. Johnson's socially liberal brand of Conservatism appealed in particular to London's suburban middle classes. His election, however, coincided with the credit crunch-driven recession with his term defined by an immediate and increasingly tight squeeze on public-sector expenditure. The future of any strategic engagement with design was thus in the balance once again, while the boroughs looked set to pare back their services to the statutory legal minimum, outside of which fell design services, public realm investment, and enhanced public space management.

The Second Mayor

It was clear from the start that Johnson's interest in planning,

design and regeneration was limited. He was elected to the mayoralty after a campaign that revealed little focus on design issues. The overriding emphasis was on leafy outer London, with Johnson strongly criticising the London Plan as 'a Zone 1 plan' (although in fact he changed it little). Thus instead of 100 new public spaces, Johnson promised 10,000 new street trees and the protection of large back gardens from the types of development that had been raising densities across London.

The new mayor quickly set about dismantling some of the public space programmes of his predecessor. An early cut was the flagship Parliament Square Improvement Project (a Livingstone priority), the planned regeneration of the only other space directly managed by the mayor. The mayor put the decision into poetic language: 'This scheme would have turned a green glade of heroes into a vast, blasted, chewing-gummed piazza. … There is absolutely no sense in Londoners paying £18 million from their already stretched transport budget in order to reduce capacity on London's roads.'[1]

The decision was revealing, demonstrating two key tensions in debates about London's public space. First, between space for traffic versus space for pedestrians. The late 1990s and early 2000s had seen some reclaiming and civilising of space for pedestrians through schemes such as the Millennium and Golden Jubilee Bridges over the Thames, and the streetscape scheme at Kensington High Street. A second tension concerned that between the continental paved piazza view of public space and the British garden square view. While the continental view of the design and use of public space had been a critical influence on the urban renaissance, for Johnson (and others) this said little about London, the cradle of the garden square. The announcement on Parliament Square was quickly followed by

Parliament Square
Despite its significance as a place of democracy and demonstration, Parliament Square remains a very grand roundabout.

THE NEW MAYOR QUICKLY SET ABOUT DISMANTLING SOME OF THE PUBLIC SPACE PROGRAMMES OF HIS PREDECESSOR. AN EARLY CUT WAS THE FLAGSHIP PARLIAMENT SQUARE IMPROVEMENT PROJECT

winding up the 100 Public Spaces programme, a move that was widely condemned by practitioners of all persuasions.

The Great Spaces Initiative

Yet, after the initial bonfire of the public space initiatives, 10 months into his mayoralty Johnson launched his own Great Spaces initiative, followed, 18 months in, by a set of new policy documents. Great Spaces was billed as 'an initiative to revitalise the capital's unique public spaces'. On the face of it, it seemed remarkably similar to the 100 Public Spaces programme it replaced, but with a greater focus on outer London, while Livingstone argued it was simply a cynical attempt to cover the retreat on the whole public space agenda.

The initiative was certainly far less ambitious than its predecessor, and instead of advancing new proposals that the mayor would take a key role in, it largely aimed at celebrating and supporting work already going on across London to improve public space. Here, it embraced projects at any stage of their development, and in so doing cleverly, or slyly (depending on one's perspective), overcame a key problem of the earlier programme which had favoured proposals in their evolutionary phase, namely the difficulty in getting schemes off the ground. Instead, schemes were carefully selected against delivery expectations and their design intentions, with successful schemes earmarked for a combination of feasibility funding, design and procurement advice, or an award as an exemplar public space. The lack of ambition was further underscored by the initial budget of £200,000 for the first year which was quickly lambasted by opposition groups on the London Assembly, including as 'great spaces on pocket money' by the former deputy mayor, Nicky Gavron. Arguably, however, the programme had

simply learned from the mistakes of its predecessor by putting the boroughs in the delivery hot seat.

Raising Standards

If Great Spaces lacked resources, a further initiative of Johnson's seemed to have a more direct, if somewhat unexpected, impact on proposals for public space. The major's emphasis from the start had been on the suburban boroughs, prioritising the protection of gardens and reducing the emphasis on the sorts of high-density solutions encouraged by his predecessor. As part of his 'Building a Better London' election manifesto, Johnson had promised to amend the London Plan to ensure the delivery of more family-sized dwellings. In characteristic style the new mayor proclaimed: 'I am not about building homes for Hobbits. … they need to be human-sized'.[2]

Backing the rhetoric, in 2010 the interim *London Housing Design Guide* was published with new housing standards for all housing in London supporting the standards already contained in the draft replacement London Plan that covered all tenures. A number of projects immediately moved away from the housing blocks that had increasingly become the norm, and looked instead to traditional urbanism solutions, including high-profile schemes such as the masterplan for bringing lasting benefits to the site of the London 2012 Olympic and Paralympic Games and the redesign of the Chelsea Barracks. In the latter, Richard Rogers' slab blocks became mired in controversy following a damning intervention by Prince Charles, and were subsequently replaced by Dixon Jones' more traditional terraces and mansion blocks around a series of green spaces. The original masterplan for how the Olympic Park would be used after the Games was also heavily criticised, this time by its client, the Olympic Park Legacy Company (OPLC),

The South Bank
With its enhanced connections to the north bank and its continuous riverside walk, the south bank of the Thames is now one of Europe's great urban walks.

'Homes for hobbits'
In the noughties, high-density and high-rise apartment blocks with small flats became the dominant development model in London, as here in Blackwall in the East End.

whose chief executive argued that it said little about London, instead presenting a series of 'high-rise and fairly bland' blocks that 'could have been anywhere'. The design U-turn, which was vocally backed by the mayor, proposes a move towards lower-rise (largely below five storeys) buildings, including family houses with gardens, around a series of Nash-inspired crescents and London squares. Post 2010, the combination of policy and circumstance looked set to presage the return of the 'traditional' garden square once again, playing directly into Boris Johnson's clear preference for traditional London vernacular. In this regard the revised housing standards are likely to have a long-term impact.

A CITY OF RENAISSANCE

The 14 years from 1997 to 2011 have seen momentous change in London, not just in the structure of its government, but in the attempt to find a new, more balanced accommodation between market and state – a 'third way'. Although neither of the chief protagonists would admit it, this was cast in a new political accommodation reminiscent, although very different from, the sort of political stability that London had enjoyed in the 1960s and 1970s. Boris Johnson, for example, noticeably sang from many of the same hymn sheets as Ken Livingstone, and adopted the substance of much of his London Plan.

However, if measured by the attraction of a city to residents, arguably an urban renaissance of the type sought by the Urban Task Force had begun in London long before the Urban Task Force, or the first mayor, commenced their work. Fundamentally this change has been driven by the sorts of capitalist ('first way') economic forces that have driven London's growth for over 2,000 years, and that are still hard at work in the city today. Nevertheless, it is probably true to say that policies from 1999

Public/private spaces
above and below: New privately owned and managed public spaces have appeared across London from the mid-1980s onwards, including these spaces at More London on the south bank of the Thames and Paddington Basin in Westminster.

THE 14 YEARS FROM 1997 TO 2011 HAVE SEEN MOMENTOUS CHANGE IN LONDON, NOT JUST IN THE STRUCTURE OF ITS GOVERNMENT, BUT IN THE ATTEMPT TO FIND A NEW, MORE BALANCED ACCOMMODATION BETWEEN MARKET AND STATE – A 'THIRD WAY'.

onwards increasingly gave regeneration processes in Central London a boost and started, in a more systematic manner, to mix environmental quality into an otherwise economically *laissez-faire* recipe for guiding London's future development.

In the public space arena, the last 14 years of London's regeneration has been a success story, but, as throughout its history, this represents the collective work of many hands, with the private sector freed, but not led, by public policy. As such London continues to show the benefits of private initiative projects and public/private partnerships – Canary Wharf, Paddington Basin, King's Cross, Stratford City and Greenwich Peninsular, among others – with new public spaces typically funded as a by-product of the development process.

The public space initiatives of both mayors were in this mode: incremental and more than a little ad hoc, although Livingstone's intervention at Trafalgar Square, the direct provision of new public space by a small minority of boroughs (such as Kensington and Chelsea), and of course the Olympic Park, demonstrate that 'second way' provision for purely social purposes in a city in which the public sector still owns and manages the vast majority of the public realm is not entirely dead. The 100 Public Spaces initiative, however, only helped to confirm that responsibility for public space in London in the first decade of the 21st century remained hopelessly fragmented and, given the size and prominence of the city, significantly under-resourced; a reality reflected in Great Spaces.

Despite this, what had been achieved in the first 10 years of the GLA has been a growing culture of concern for urban design in London, in which both mayors (alongside central government) have played a significant role, although this has more often played out in their policy and regulatory roles than in the direct provision of public space projects. The support of the mayor's small design team (Design for London) added weight to this effort and it has been influential in helping to shape some of the capital's recent successful public space projects, including Acton Town Square (2006), Potters Fields (2007) and Barking Town Square (2009). Nevertheless, mayors (of whichever colour) remain reliant on the boroughs and private actors to deliver much of the design agenda and, at that level, interest and expertise in such issues remains highly variable. Sometimes 'third way', sometimes 'second', but typically 'first way'; this, it seems, is the 'London way'. ⌂

Notes
1. Quoted in BBC News, 'Parliament Piazza Plan Scrapped', 2008; see http://news.bbc.co.uk/1/hi/england/london/7547311.stm.
2. Quoted in F Hamilton, 'Boris Johnson to End London's Hobbit Habit with 50,000 New Homes', 2008; see http://www.timesonline.co.uk/tol/news/politics/article5198945.ece.

Barking Town Square
bottom: Barking Town Square was the result of a public/private partnership in which Design for London played a crucial role.

14

THE NUMBER OF YEARS THAT SAW NEW APPROACHES TO LONDON'S DESIGN

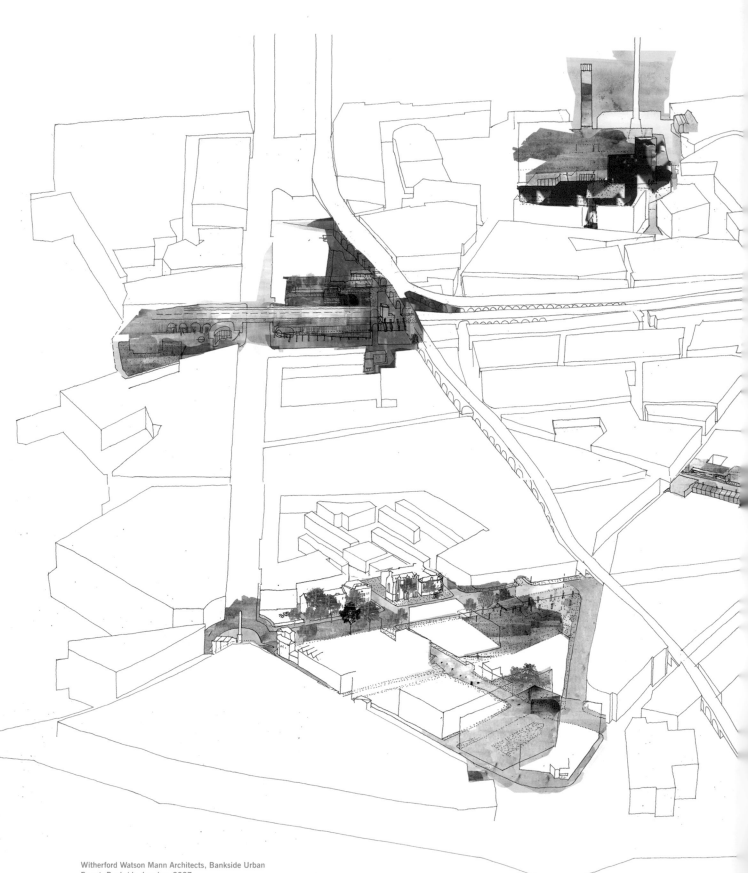

Witherford Watson Mann Architects, Bankside Urban Forest, Bankside, London, 2007
'Place of Exchange' diagram highlighting the key social hubs within Bankside: from cathedral, university and art gallery to schools and retail clusters.

David Littlefield

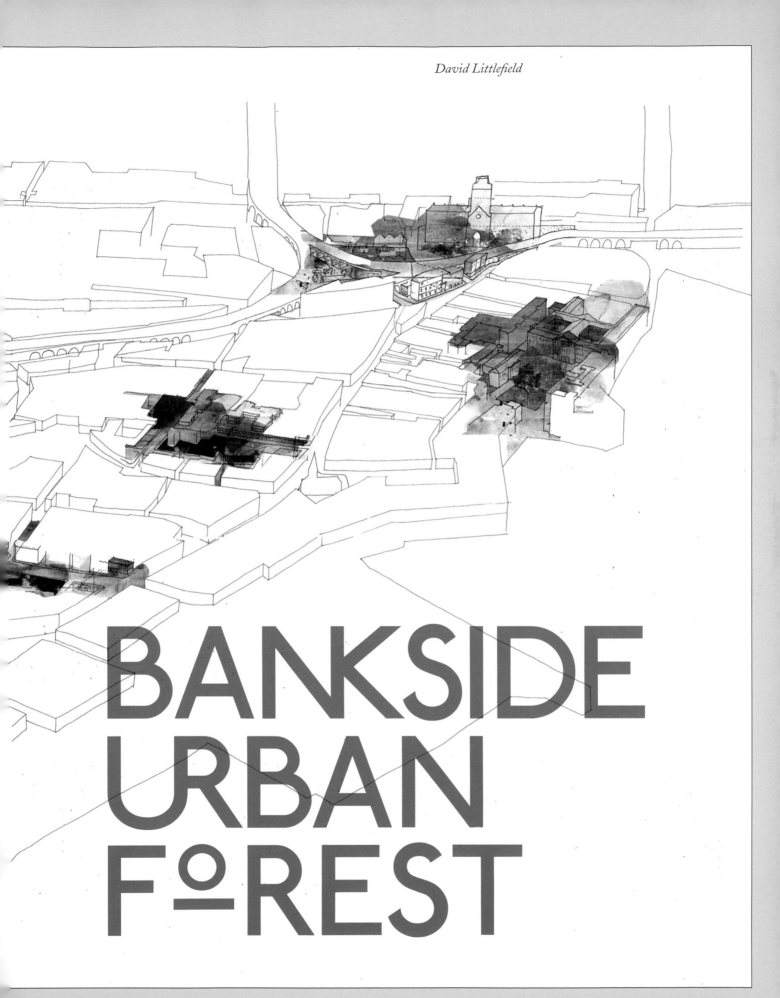

BANKSIDE URBAN FOREST

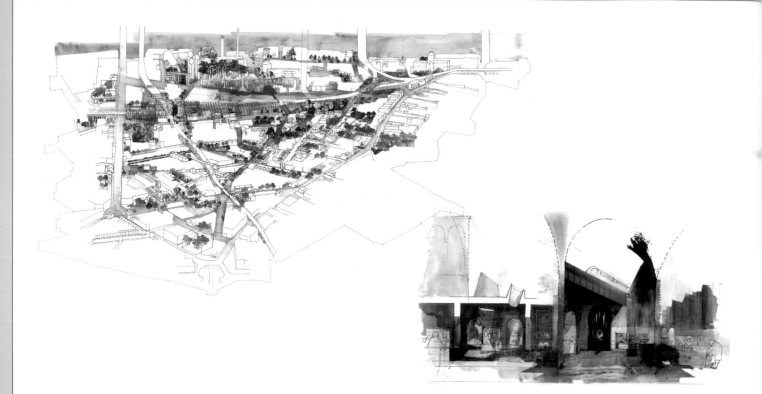

Drawing illustrating the 'meshing' of the active edges and the urban interior; the large institutions begin to link with the quieter inner core, while the interior is altered enough to invite exploration.

Bankside is characterised by railway viaducts that add both charm and a sense of danger to the neighbourhood. The railway arches have the potential to provide increased connections through the site or offer space for small businesses.

Bankside Urban Forest is a long-term, multi-agency, community-based project that aims to preserve and enhance the qualities of Bankside while recognising the need for change and the arrival of institutional newcomers. Loosely bounded by the Thames in the north, Elephant and Castle in the south, Blackfriars Road to the west and Borough High Street to the east, this district is characterised by high-energy edges of global commerce and tourism and a quiet urban interior. The notion of an urban forest has been developed by Witherford Watson Mann Architects to provide a framework within which all development across the area can be coordinated while seeking to preserve a sense of the site's unique identity.

The idea of the forest is only semi-literal. It does involve a degree of greening, but the architects have deployed it metaphorically also – looking for 'rides, streams and clearings'. Rides are the long, straight routes cut through forests, manifested here as principal streets; streams are the meandering pathways; clearings are represented by those moments where one stops, such as pocket parks or larger

openings, which could be recognised as 'places'. A series of studies and community consultations, carried out since 2006, have managed to capture (through maps, photography, diagrams and text) something of the identity of Bankside, its opportunities for investment and the qualities prized by local people. Further, by bringing together all development projects, the intention is to make best use of Section 106 funds (planning gain) and other opportunities for cross-investment. That way, high-profile projects might stand a better chance of integration into the wider place, rather than standing aloof. Benefits might also flow to the community, rather than leave local people as bystanders.

'Rather like an organ transplant, the host environment can sometimes reject or turn its back on the new development, leaving it isolated, or requiring it to take the form of an enclave community,' writes Ken Worpole in the project framework document.[1] The urban forest is based on the idea that those responsible for regeneration schemes have to appreciate the very real benefits that flow the other way, from the host

southwark bridge road

union street →

Concept drawing for Flat Iron Square, a project completed in 2011;
a reinvention of a small urban island by altering the traffic layout,
improving pedestrian connectivity and tree planting.

community to the new development and its inhabitants and users. Thus the forest slowly encroaches on the new development and integrates it by degrees into the historic ecology of the terrain. So rather than Southwark residents feeling that their fine-grain pattern of urban living and community is going to be crushed by high-rise development bestriding the whole area, the urban forest strategy builds on the richness and intimacy of the existing communities, integrating the new developments at Bankside into the wider urban fabric.

Significantly, this low-key regeneration project has established strong community support for change, partly by emphasising the qualities of existing street patterns and spatial qualities, and partly by levering in money for enhancement schemes that might otherwise have never penetrated this quiet interior. Principles of evolutionary change and sharing underpin the work. Budgets are relatively modest (in the region of £7 million), but dozens of small-scale projects have been identified that could make very real differences to the local community and visitors: traffic control, better road crossings, public art, benches, canopies, tree planting, clearer cycle paths and the marking of spatial thresholds by, for example, transforming a viaduct into a 'furry arch' through vertical planting.

Administered by the London Borough of Southwark, Design for London and Better Bankside, the project involves a wide variety of partners including the Cross River Partnership, Tate Modern, Land Securities, the Architecture Foundation and Transport for London. ⌂

Note
1. www.betterbankside.co.uk/bankside-urban-forest.

holland street

← sumner street →

Proposal for a playground adjacent to Tate Modern, characterised by Scots pines and diagonal pathways.

Concept scheme for Redcross Gardens, making it a 'place of exchange' with improved traffic management.

redcross way

little dorrit court →

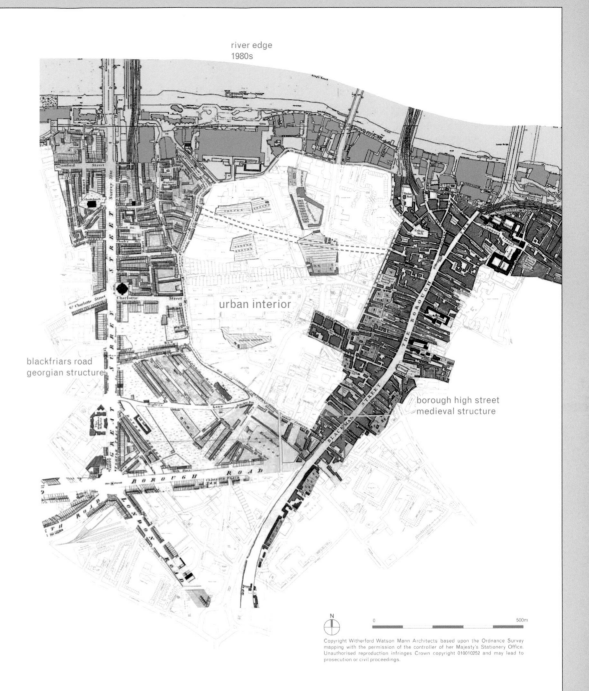

river edge
1980s

urban interior

blackfriars road
georgian structure

borough high street
medieval structure

Image of the 'urban interior' illustrating the disconnection between the heavily used, high-intensity periphery of the development site and its quieter interior.

N

0   500m

Copyright Witherford Watson Mann Architects based upon the Ordnance Survey mapping with the permission of the controller of her Majesty's Stationery Office. Unauthorised reproduction infringes Crown copyright 010010252 and may lead to prosecution or civil proceedings.

So rather than Southwark residents feeling that their fine-grain pattern of urban living and community is going to be crushed by high-rise development bestriding the whole area, the urban forest strategy builds on the richness and intimacy of the existing communities, integrating the new developments at Bankside into the wider urban fabric.

NEO
BANKSIDE

2016 ESTIMATED YEAR THAT MOST OF INNER LONDON WILL NO LONGER BE AFFORDABLE TO LOW-INCOME TENANTS

Rogers Stirk Harbour + Partners, NEO Bankside, Bankside, London, 2011–
The project will be a new exclusive enclave that exacerbates social polarisation in London and is unrelated to local planning or housing needs.

Beyond the City's walls, Southwark was for hundreds of years one of the capital's liveliest boroughs: London's industrial backyard and entertainment district. It was the site of Shakespeare's Globe Theatre and the Vauxhall Pleasure Gardens as well as several prisons, such as the Marshalsea. However, it fell into decline in the late 20th century as print works and the London docks closed. **Matthew Gandy** describes a new development in Southwark, adjacent to Tate Modern, which marks its reinvention as a luxurious enclave for the internationally rich.

The summer 2011 edition of the glossy *Tate Etc* magazine contains a double-page advertisement for a new housing development next to Tate Modern entitled NEO Bankside. 'Move in next door to Warhol, Dalí and Picasso,' reads the text, and 'brush shoulders with some illustrious arty types'. Designed by Rogers Stirk Harbour + Partners, in partnership with the developers Native Land and Grosvenor, this set of four residential pavilions is the latest in a series of ultra-exclusive housing projects being built across London.

NEO Bankside replaces an earlier plan for the site – the infamous 33-storey Tate Tower – which was defeated in 2002 by vociferous local opposition from the Tate gallery along with nearby residents in other exclusive developments such as Bankside Lofts.[1] A phalanx of high-profile people have been enlisted for the promotion of NEO Bankside, as reflected in a nine-minute film on the project website entitled *NEO Bankside and the Neighbourhood* which plays extensively on the

'working character' of Bankside in London's industrial past and the recent cultural regeneration of the area.[2] Most critically, however, a project of this kind could not have occurred without the very extensive public investment that has taken place in Bankside since the 1990s as part of urban regeneration efforts in deprived parts of inner London.

The exterior of the four pavilions is encased in a lattice of 'external bracing' that references the late-Modern facades of the Lloyd's Building, the Centre Pompidou and other architectural exoskeletons from Richard Rogers' past. The interior of the show apartment has a pokey feel despite its claimed size. The large windows cannot disguise its single aspect – one is conscious of standing in a larger space that has been spliced into two apartments – and the layout is consumed by a proliferation of corridors and en suite bathrooms. The design is reminiscent of what JG Ballard terms 'American interiors' characterised by 'overly spacious kitchens' and 'complete physical privacy'.[3] Perhaps the oddest feature of all, however, is a triangular slither of enclosed space, produced by the subdivision of the building, which is described as a 'winter garden' with a 'temperate semi-external environment'. The intended clientele for these apartments, which are priced at between £1 million and £5 million, is hinted at in the promotional literature with its very extensive list of exclusive features ranging from a state-of the-art wine cellar and 'richly landscaped gardens' to a standard of concierge service 'normally associated with five-star hotels'. The development must surely be aimed principally at overseas buyers from markets such as the Middle East, the super-rich of the former Soviet Union, or parts of east Asia that have remained relatively unscathed through the most recent episode of global economic turbulence. The market for these and other similar luxury developments is inextricably linked to new patterns of wealth inequality and tax evasion within the global economy.[4]

In order to really evaluate the significance of NEO Bankside, it needs to be viewed in a broader context. Whatever

This slither of space between two apartments is described as a 'winter garden'.

Interior of a NEO Bankside show apartment. Old Vic artistic director Kevin Spacey was the narrator for a promotional film for the development; his image remains eerily frozen on the flat-screen TV.

the apparent cultural or ecological novelty of the project, this is a venture very much rooted in old money, landed privilege and centuries of residential exclusivity in London, as indicated by the partnership between the developers Native Land and Grosvenor, who already own significant parts of Central and West London and boast assets of over £10 billion. Yet it also reflects a glaring dislocation within the London housing market between the actual needs of ordinary Londoners and the impact of global social and economic factors on patterns of investment for the internationally wealthy.

NEO Bankside represents a colossal misappropriation of resources at a time of intensifying housing shortages in London. Richard Rogers, the 2007 Pritzker Architecture Prize Laureate, has been closely associated with recent debates over urban sustainability through his 1995 BBC Reith lectures 'Cities for a small planet', his role as Chair of the UK Government's Urban Task Force in 1998, and more recently as Chief Adviser on 'architecture and urbanism' to the former Mayor of London, Ken Livingstone. With these impressive credentials it seems impossible to believe that this proposed development is an anomaly or a mistake: it rather reveals the hubris of contemporary architectural discourse as espoused by Rogers and many of his contemporaries.

The core dynamic behind London's housing crisis has been the failure to build enough social housing because political and economic priorities have lain elsewhere. Terms such as 'affordable housing' obscure the fact that most of London's households cannot afford to buy their own home and must therefore rent accommodation wherever they can find it. With recent changes in government policy to reduce rent subsidies and further choke off the availability of social housing, there will be a forced exodus of the poor out of inner London. By 2016 it is estimated that most of inner London will no longer be affordable to low-income tenants, and those outlying areas that do remain affordable will be marked by intensifying concentrations of deprivation and unemployment.[5]

The character of London is changing and projects such as NEO Bankside are connected to the wider transformation of the city into an increasingly segregated and polarised metropolis. In 1999, the Urban Task Force, chaired by Rogers, published the influential document *Towards an Urban Renaissance*, which began with a mission statement calling for 'a new vision of urban regeneration founded on the principles of design excellence, social well-being and environmental responsibility'.[6] Rogers and his colleagues decried how 'we have lost ownership of our towns and cities, allowing them to become spoilt by poor design, economic dispersal and social polarisation'.[7] The construction of NEO Bankside, some 11 years later, reveals the apotheosis of this market-led vision for urban regeneration where issues of social inclusion or design quality have been repeatedly subsumed behind vacuous slogans or obfuscatory rhetoric. ᐰ

Notes
1. Andrew Harris, 'Livingstone Versus Serota: The High-Rise Battle of Bankside', *The London Journal*, Vol 33, No 3, November 2008, pp 289–99.
2. The promotional film for Neo-Bankside opens with Kevin Spacey, the artistic director of the Old Vic, followed by a litany of powerful local figures such as Ian Hislop of Tate Modern, Peter Kyle of the Shakespeare Globe and Jude Kelly of the South Bank Centre.
3. JG Ballard, *Miracles of Life*, Harper Perennial (London), 2008.
4. Nicholas Shaxson, *Treasure Islands: Tax Havens and the Men Who Stole the World*, Bodley Head (London), 2010.
5. See: Cambridge Centre for Housing & Planning Research, *How Will Changes to Local Housing Allowance Affect Low-Income Tenants in Private Rented Housing?*, Cambridge Centre for Housing & Planning Research (Cambridge) 2010; Cambridge Centre for Housing & Planning Research, *Housing Benefit Reform and the Spatial Segregation of Low-Income Households in London,* Cambridge Centre for Housing & Planning Research (Cambridge), 2011.
6. Urban Task Force, *Towards an Urban Renaissance*, Report of the Urban Task Force chaired by Lord Rogers of Riverside, Department of Environment, Transport and the Regions (London), 1999, p 1.
7. Ibid, p 2.

An idealised living space as shown in the advertising hoardings for NEO Bankside. Note the scattering of art books by the window and the pastoral idyll between the towers.

NEO BANKSIDE REPRESENTS A COLOSSAL MISAPPROPRIATION OF RESOURCES AT A TIME OF INTENSIFYING HOUSING SHORTAGES IN LONDON.

Michael Batty

URBAN REGENERATION AS SELF-ORGANISATION

Michael Batty redefines regeneration within the context of a wider system of urban reproduction. A spontaneous response to self-organisation, regeneration is a force that can just as easily manifest itself in dereliction and decline. As part of a bottom-up system, what role can there be for intervention by designers and policy-makers? Batty suggests how urban planning needs to identify key points where small change can lead to massive change for the better, so as 'to plant seeds that do not fall on stony ground'.

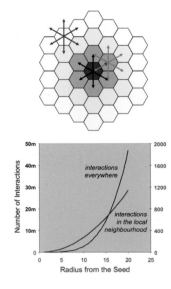

Figure 1. How a seed planted in the urban landscape influences its neighbours by diffusing its success (or otherwise) through interactions.

Cities are living, self-organising systems that grow organically from the bottom up. They are composed of entities – people and buildings – that have limited lifespans and have to be renewed continuously. Indeed, regeneration is the hallmark of any living system, and in cities, most activity that takes place can be considered as part of this process of renewal. New growth or absolute decay tends to be a relatively small proportion of the total change. Cities are continually in flux as people and their activities respond incessantly to changed circumstances that involve shifts in movement patterns, locations, the use of buildings and in social preferences.

Whether or not the processes of regeneration are sustainable and lead to a better quality of life is not assured simply because a city reproduces itself. Cities change through positive feedback. Change builds on itself and, if there is growth or decline, regeneration might reinforce the cycle, each wave of change building on the previous, often spreading out as well as polarising through intricate patterns of diffusion. Growth is easier to track as a positive feedback, good examples being gentrification where one group, usually the richer, takes over the buildings that were once occupied by the poorer, thus pricing out the resident population. The most visible example of this type of cumulative causation leading to a massive decline is the vacating of the city of Detroit, which has fallen in population from 1.4 million in 1970 to half that today, with the consequent abandonment of whole areas of the inner city and a greening of what were once prosperous residential areas.

(Re)defining (Re)generation

A key feature of systems that regenerate themselves is that they do so spontaneously. To do so otherwise would require control of every basic element of the system, and it thus follows that systems of any complexity must affect self-regeneration through self-organisation from the bottom up. In city planning, regeneration has come to mean something a little different. Urban regeneration is now usually structured through planned interventions that are anything but spontaneous, and often conflict with processes that are intrinsic to the survival of the system itself. Sometimes spontaneous regeneration can be stopped in its tracks by attempts at planned regeneration, which tends to be manufactured from the top down. A city is composed of layer upon layer of interactions that represent a multiplexing of networks acting to deliver energy, information, materials and people to its parts in such a way that the networks contain great redundancy. If fractured, cities usually continue to work because of the enormous redundancy that is built into their fabric through multiple networks, alternative, complementary locations and ways of working, although if their key hubs are attacked they will break down. In the same way, if they become overloaded, their networks jam, but in general, because cities operate from the bottom up through the actions of millions of individuals, they tend to adjust easily and quickly to changed circumstances.

Figure 1 shows in abstract terms how such processes generate positive feedbacks as spirals of prosperity or decline that diffuse across the urban landscape. An idealised urban landscape is broken into regular cells or locations where activity can be located, with the arrows indicating how adjacent cells influence one another. When a seed of growth is planted, say the central red cell in Figure 1, cells around it become activated and the innovation diffuses as waves: the red cell generates orange, the orange yellow, the yellow beige, and so on. The number of cells and the number of interactions – in this case six for each cell – grow approximately in proportion to the area of the circle πr^2. This exponential effect is even more powerful – it is super-exponential – if each cell influences every other in the growing system, with the graph showing how this positive feedback simulates the spread of influence. This is what we hope for of regeneration, for as areas regenerate spontaneously their 'DNA' causes the cell to 'grow' to form other cells.

In an equivalent way, Figure 1 has a mirror image as a process of decline with a bad cell affecting its neighbours and in turn making them 'bad'. This is much more akin to the way industries begin to decline, with one industry failing and destroying the linkages to neighbouring industries, often leading to a spiral of deindustrialisation. There is also uncertainty as to how much the seed affects its neighbours, and if this is built into the model diffusion becomes more random.

As the life of any activity comes to an end, it needs to be renewed. The wave-like structure of regeneration that occurs as old activity is replaced with new is also subject to uncertainty and ultimately the original structuring of the city in areas of like development is destroyed through differential renewal, thus mixing land uses. The theoretical logic for this process is explained as part of the logic of complexity theory,[1] and the practical applicability of the idea is demonstrated by Nabeel Hamdi.[2] A picture of this process can be seen in Figure 2, which is a simple version of the model shown in Figure 1. It breeds wave after wave of regeneration which successively mix the cells in terms of the time when they are developed, making it harder and harder to detect what influenced what as the initial structuring washes itself away in the resultant mix.[3]

The trick for urban planning is to identify key points where small change can lead spontaneously to massive change for the better.[4] We need to figure out ways to plant seeds that do not fall on stony ground, leading to regeneration that is sustainable from the bottom up, avoiding more and more investment from the top down. Growth as well as decline can be pathological and urban sprawl is often regarded as unsustainable. However, it is inner-city decline in areas that once housed industries whose equivalents are now highly automated and footloose, requiring little labour, that fall into vicious cycles of progressive decline that are hard to break. Areas of such decline are to be found in most large cities where their industrial base has gone, only to be replaced with financial services and high tech, located elsewhere. Indeed, the proposal to locate the Olympic Park – the heart of the London 2012 Olympic and Paralympic Games – in East London is primarily because there is much vacant, abandoned land. However, much of the land is contaminated and over the last 20 years there has been enormous investment in the area, which has led to little.[5]

The mission now is to attempt an even bigger wave of planned regeneration which will kick in after the event has taken place, for it is the lasting benefits of the Games that are crucial to the regeneration.[6] In a sense, to enable little seeds of growth to do their work, the current project is to provide the right kind of conditions (in the soil) in which regeneration can work its magic. Most of these seeds are envisaged to be privately funded, and thus it is generally regarded that large-scale development and

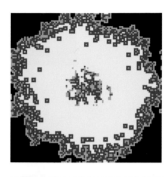

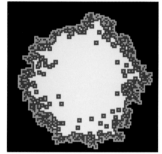

Figure 2. Successive waves of growth and then regeneration wash away the initial structure (top) to generate a mix (bottom).

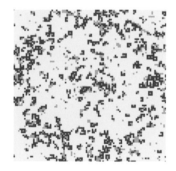

The mission now is to attempt an even bigger wave of planned regeneration which will kick in after the event has taken place, for it is the lasting benefits of the Games that are crucial to the regeneration.

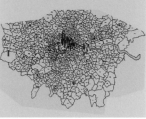

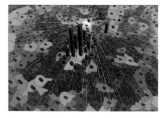

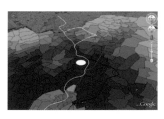

extensive site preparation are required if private development is to have the flexibility to flourish.

Identifying Critical Points for Intervention

Regeneration is part of the process of enabling the city's various networks to keep functioning, and declining areas that we might consider problematic are key to the processes of natural regeneration. If we interfere in them without understanding all the possible ramifications, such planned regeneration can be disastrous, leading to exactly the opposite effects than those intended. The causes of decline and poverty usually relate to industries that have long outlived their usefulness. The spiral of decline that sets in further impoverishes the remaining population as the youngest and brightest leave, and with an ageing population and workforce such areas become increasingly unattractive for new industries and services. Many regeneration proposals simply try to address these issues by providing new property-led infrastructure that is everything but a new basis for jobs. Housing is one of the classic remedies, but all this succeeds in doing is providing updated residential facilities for the same population.

The key is to find the right mix of activities, to plant seeds that lead to the regeneration attracting related activities because of their evident synergy. This does not necessarily require large-scale investments, but it does require activities that lead to new synergies. In fact, large-scale infrastructure projects are probably the wrong types of activity for regeneration because the jobs they bring tend to be few – simply for building and then maintaining the infrastructure. In East London, all of the activities to date prior to the Games (with the exception of the Jubilee Line extension linking Stratford to the City) have all been modest investments. The Olympic Park site will provide massive infrastructure whose success will be after the Games are ended when the stadia are used for high-profile sports events and the shopping-centre complex will continue to attract people into the area.

The biggest dangers, however, are that though people will come into the area to shop and use the facilities, much of the expenditure they generate will not benefit the local community. If one provides infrastructure and facilities for people to come to a place, they can equally well leave a place using that same infrastructure. East London's proximity to the City of London is a major advantage and there are already some evident spillovers, but it is surprising that there have not been more, given house price differentials. Nevertheless, a parallel agenda in social reconstruction and the provision of better services by the local authorities involved could well resolve some of these potential difficulties.[7]

Tracing the Impacts

The multipliers that ripple through the city, which are expressed in both physical terms as networks and less visible social and information interactions, condition the extent to which we can explore how effective regeneration might be. The Centre for Advanced Spatial Analysis (CASA) has built a land-use transportation model of how populations relate to employment, largely in terms of simulating the journey to work and to shop. Here, the city is divided up into small zones, like the cells in Figures 1 and 2, and the key urban networks are built through the various transportation modes – road, Tube, bus and heavy rail – that link them together. There is a long tradition of building models of this kind that largely look at the impact of new transportation proposals, but this extended model allows us to ask many 'what if?' questions. For example: What will be the impact of locating 100,000 new jobs in the Olympic Park area, which is what the London Borough of Newham is predicting for the next 20 years.[8] If this many jobs do materialise, there is no doubt that there will be an enormous regeneration on the scale of the London Docklands, but the key question is will they materialise, and if they do will the associated population live locally or commute in from elsewhere? Some jobs will be pump primed, but most will need to be generated spontaneously.

One of the other big infrastructure projects is Crossrail, which is designed to link West to East London by 2015. Whether or not a greater proportion of the population will drift west even though there are new jobs in the east is a critical question that the CASA model is designed to answer. A visual walkthrough of how these impacts might be assessed using data from the model in map and 3-D form begins in Figure 3, which shows the highly concentrated pattern of employment across London with Stratford marked out. In Figure 4, all this data has been imported into Google Earth showing employment as a bar map, population density, and the transport flows into the Stratford hub. The proximity of the City is evident in terms of jobs, and the advantages of the area are graphically demonstrated in Figure 5, which shows the relative accessibility – nearness of places to one another (highest red to lowest blue) overlaid with the Tube lines that serve the area.

The key to assessing the regeneration is to develop a series of scenarios where we plug new jobs, homes, retailing and transport links into the area and then predict what the impact will be. Various scenarios can be developed in this way, and here we will develop two: first, simply locating 50,000 jobs and the current planned housing into the key cells around Stratford and then doing the same by adding twice that many jobs – 100,000 – putting in the planned Crossrail from West London into the area, and adding new retail employment, already approved and planned. In Figure 6, the jobs are simply plugged in to show the population that is generated and redistributed by this regeneration. In essence, what we need to demonstrate is that the population that is generated from these jobs stays largely in the area and does not move out to what are historically more attractive areas. What happens, of course, is that populations not only grow through these new jobs, but the existing population redistributes in response to the changed urban landscape with losses in some areas as well as gains overall.

Figure 7 shows that although the scale of these jobs and the new housing leads to largest absolute changes in population across East London, when the percentage change is examined, apart from a small area in Stratford itself population leaks to more prosperous areas southwest of the centre. There is population loss in the centre itself due to congestion charging still working itself out, and the concentration of transport links in the corridor between the City and Stratford is shown in Figure 8. But it is when the second scenario is tested, adding 100,000 jobs, building Crossrail and locating retailing and housing in the area that the real problems emerge. As can be seen in Figure 9, Crossrail (shown in Figure 10) tends to draw

Figure 6. The location of new jobs and housing in East London and relative shifts in population. The black bar is 50,000 jobs in Stratford, while the red and blue bars are gains and losses in population due to a restructuring across the metropolis.

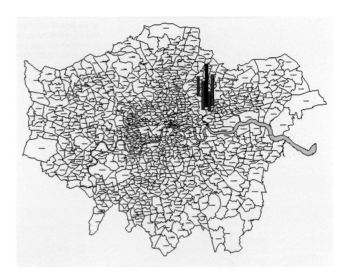

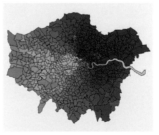

Figure 7. Mixed blessings: Absolute larger gains in population in East London due to regeneration, but relative percentage gains in West London. These maps reflect a ranking of population gains from highest rank (red) to lowest (blue). The top map shows that, in general, the east gains the most population, despite a shadow to the immediate southeast of Stratford, but the map below shows that relative gains tend to be higher in inner West London and along the Central Line, despite the highest relative gain being in the immediate vicinity of Stratford.

Hattie Hartman

OLYMPI
STRAT

Olympic Park Legacy Company (OPLC), Visualisation of Olympic Park in Legacy
View looking south towards Canary Wharf with the Velodrome and Olympic and Paralympic Village (left), the Olympic Stadium and Anish Kapoor's ArcelorMittal Orbit tower (centre distance), and the International Broadcast Centre (right).

9.6 NUMBER OF KILOMETRES BETWEEN WESTMINSTER AND THE OLYMPIC PARK

Allies & Morrison, Olympic Park Games Masterplan Study, Stratford, London, 2004
An early masterplan study with new bridges highlighted in red. Although Stratford had good external transport connections beyond the site, the Olympic Park site itself was poorly connected to surrounding communities on either side of the Lea River Valley. The design for the Park includes more than 30 new bridges, many with temporary sections that will be removed after the London 2012 Olympic and Paralympic Games, which link across waterways, motorways and railways, connecting communities across the valley for the first time.

Aerial view of Olympic Park site prior to redevelopment, Stratford, London, 2005
When London won the bid in 2005, the site of the future Olympic Park was bisected by waterways and transport infrastructure and occupied by more than 200 buildings.

East London is undergoing radical change. The London 2012 Olympic and Paralympic Games, situated 9.6 kilometres (6 miles) east of Westminster in the Lower Lea Valley, are transforming the landscape of some of the city's most deprived communities.

The 200-hectare (494-acre) site straddles four boroughs that for decades served as London's backyard. In contrast with West London's affluent housing estates and leafy parks, East London, closer to the mouth of the Thames, was traditionally home to the city's docks and suffered serious economic decline with the rise of containerisation in the late 1960s.

Crisscrossed with transport and utility infrastructure by the turn of the century, the post-industrial site was a backwater, occupied by some 200 small businesses, an active allotment community and a cycleway. Dumping grounds for obsolete appliances lined abandoned canals overgrown with abundant vegetation. Ironically, though parts of the site were derelict and contaminated, it had the elements of a precious green lung in a part of the city devoid of open space. Bisected by the river Lea, minimal east–west connections linked the two sides of the valley. The Channel Tunnel Rail Link (CTRL), completed

in 2003 with a station in adjacent Stratford, transformed the area's prospects. Nearby Stratford Regional station serves two underground lines and the Docklands Light Railway, as well as National Rail and London Overground lines. Recognising this development potential prior to the bid for the London 2012 Olympic and Paralympic Games, a consortium led by Stanhope assembled 29 hectares (72 acres) – primarily former railway yards – for a major retail and commercial complex adjacent to Stratford station.

As the idea of a London bid gained momentum in 2002/03, the East London site offered a conjunction of relatively vacant land with excellent transport, essential for access to an Olympic Park site. Then mayor Ken Livingstone was adamant that if London was to host the Games, the multibillion-pound investment should be utilised to improve the lives of East Londoners. Regeneration was the premise from the outset. In an Olympic first, a legacy masterplan to ensure lasting benefits for the area after the Games was developed simultaneously with the masterplan for the Games as the bid was prepared.

The crux of London's proposal, masterplanned initially by the EDAW (now AECOM) consortium, is a sinuous parkland

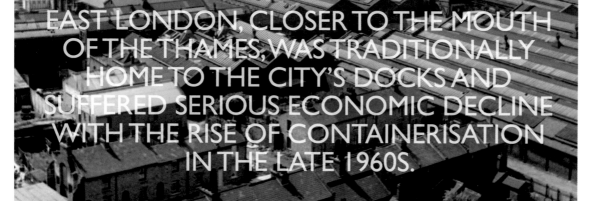

EAST LONDON, CLOSER TO THE MOUTH OF THE THAMES, WAS TRADITIONALLY HOME TO THE CITY'S DOCKS AND SUFFERED SERIOUS ECONOMIC DECLINE WITH THE RISE OF CONTAINERISATION IN THE LATE 1960S.

Stratford Railway Yard, Stratford, London, c 1970
Transport infrastructure was a major factor in the selection of the Stratford site for the Games, and approximately £7 billion has been invested in long-term improvements to public transport. Stratford Regional station serves three underground lines, as well as the Docklands Light Railway and Network Rail. Nearby Stratford International provides direct connections to St Pancras and Europe.

that enhances the waterways and ecology of the Lea River Valley. Extensive works to the Park will take place in 2012–13, doubling the amount of Metropolitan Open Space from about 50 hectares (123 acres) during the Games to 102 hectares (252 acres), just under the size of Kensington Gardens. All venue and infrastructure investments have been validated by their long-term viability. After the Games, five sporting venues will remain in the Park; all other structures are temporary.

More than sporting venues, affordable housing and jobs are critical for kick-starting regeneration. In addition to 2,800 units of housing (50 per cent affordable) that will be converted from the Olympic and Paralympic Village, the masterplan allows for up to 11,000 units of additional housing when fully developed. The International Broadcast Centre/Main Press Centre, home to 20,000 journalists during the Games, will provide 90,000 square metres (968,752 square feet) of commercial space afterwards, and is envisioned as a hub for digital media and creative industries. Westfield shopping centre, located just south of Stratford station on what was originally part of Stanhope's Stratford City site, opened in September 2011 with an anticipated 9,000 jobs.

The regeneration track record of past Olympic Games is mixed. Although espoused by almost every candidate city, Barcelona (1992) is the only one that managed to seize the momentum of Olympic investment to meaningfully regenerate a dilapidated area of the city. London's approach of legacy first is promising. Six fringe masterplans developed in tandem with the Olympic Park since 2006 and supported by approximately £80 million investment in public realm projects endeavour to physically link the Park with surrounding communities and facilitate joined-up thinking between boroughs. City-making at this scale requires decades. The new Queen Elizabeth Olympic Park provides a strong foundation for regeneration, yet even the best masterplan is subject to the vagaries of the property market and the imponderables of political will. Δ

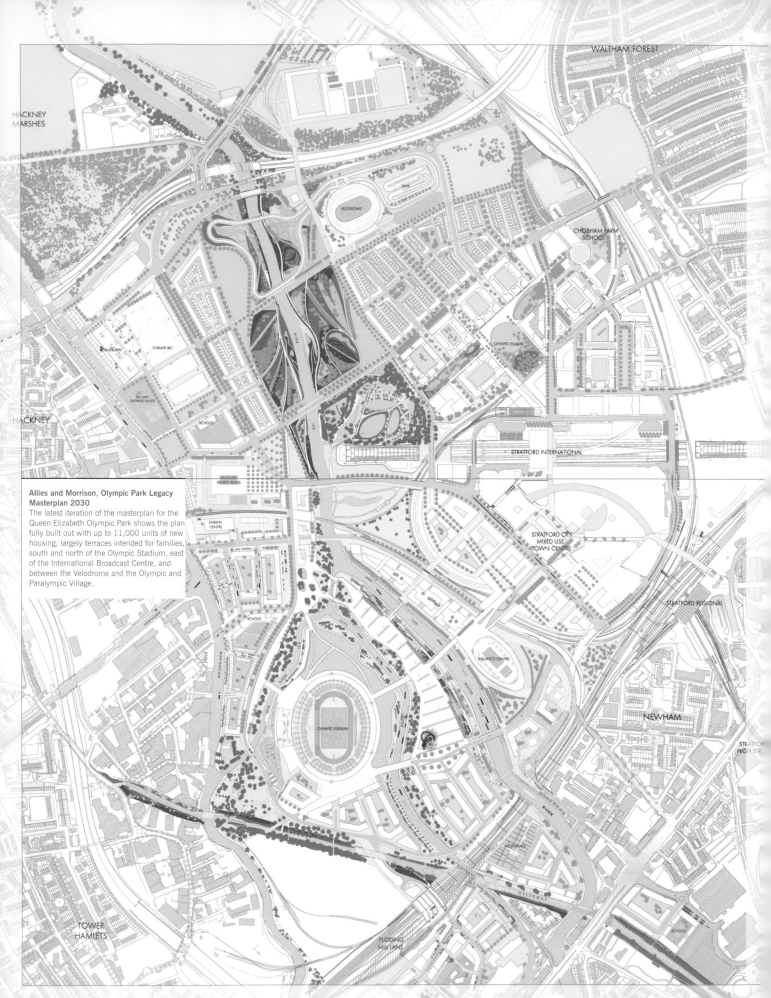

Allies and Morrison, Olympic Park Legacy Masterplan 2030
The latest iteration of the masterplan for the Queen Elizabeth Olympic Park shows the plan fully built out with up to 11,000 units of new housing, largely terraces intended for families, south and north of the Olympic Stadium, east of the International Broadcast Centre, and between the Velodrome and the Olympic and Paralympic Village.

WALTHAM FOREST

HACKNEY MARSHES

EASTWAY CYCLE CIRCUIT

VELODROME

CHOBHAM FARM SCHOOL

FORMER MPC

FORMER IBC

IBC/MPC CATERING VILLAGE

SCHOOL

OLYMPIC VILLAGE

HACKNEY

MULTI-USE SPORTS VENUE

STRATFORD INTERNATIONAL

ENERGY CENTRE

STRATFORD CITY MIXED USE TOWN CENTRE

SCHOOL

STRATFORD REGIONAL

AQUATICS CENTRE

NEWHAM

OLYMPIC STADIUM

STRATFORD HIGH STR

ALLOTMENTS

RIVER

TOWER HAMLETS

SCHOOL

GREENWAY

PUDDING MILL LANE

Design for London (DfL), Emerging proposals for the Lea Valley, 2011
The Queen Elizabeth Olympic Park in the context of the green spine of the lower Lea Valley Regional Park, which stretches 42 kilometres (26 miles) from Hertfordshire to the Thames. Six Olympic Park fringe masterplans have been developed in tandem with the Games.

WHAT IS

On the 75th anniversary of Lewis Mumford's rhetorical essay 'What is a City?', **Austin Williams** asks whether we risk defining cities out of existence.

It is 75 years since the great urban theorist and historian Lewis Mumford posed the question, 'What is a City?', to which he replied that 'in its complete sense [it] is a geographical plexus, an economic organization, an institutional process, a theater of social action, and an aesthetic symbol of creative unity'.[1] In essence, it is a place of movement and flux, reflecting temporal intangibility while at the same time representing something indefinably sensate.

In 1905 the Modernist writer Ford Madox Ford posed a similar question. After completing a number of forays into and around London – by bicycle, on foot, by bus – he asked himself, 'What is London?', and replied, with remarkable candour, that he still did not know. For all his exploration, he was none the wiser and could only describe it as the 'apotheosis of modern life'[2] where change, the essence of the city, was to be recognised, celebrated and embraced.

Contrary to Mumford's celebration of movement and flux, it would seem that the contemporary condition is one of stasis and risk aversion. And instead of Ford's joyous faith in modernity and its future orientation, today it is the modern world that is frequently cited as the cause of society's ills. After all, 'future-proofing'[3] is the new urban buzzword, where the core concerns of the present seem to be to mitigate the potential harms to come. The contemporary condition of being fearful of the future and suspicious of our own motivations for wanting to get there is not the best starting point to be able to change things for the better.

In Mumford's classic *The City in History*[4] he describes the city as a place of civilisation. For him, cities caused humans to emerge from their barbarous relationship with nature and develop an ordered, cultured, social stability. Compare that with Alan Weisman's more recent, misanthropic account that complains that humans 'vainly or disingenuously pretend'[5] that civilisation has dominion over nature. It seems that in a relatively short space of time, we have gone from celebrating man's ability to creatively transcend natural barriers, to a depressingly widespread belief that human hubris is inherently, or inevitably, harmful.

As such, the physical environment has become deified; its abstraction reified. One extreme variation of this tragic agrarian mindset are CJ Lim's Smart-Cities[6] that envisage a form of spiritual salvation through urban agriculture. But even the more mainstream concept of the 'compact city' reflects the environmental anxieties and limits that dominate public debate these days.

With a less adventurous – or, some might say, a more fearful – frame of reference taking hold in society since Mumford's day, modern urban commentators and practitioners prefer to wallow in the comfort blanket of their surroundings rather than to challenge them.

This kind of Western defensiveness, materialist contrition or self-loathing concerning modernity is also reflected in a reverence for the developing world which, we are constantly informed, has much to teach us, particularly on the question of our relationship to nature, our pace of life, and a general humility towards urban development. Such naive romanticism is a common feature in writings about ubiquitous sustainable developments. Musheireb, a new town in Doha, for example, is heralded for being built at a sedate pace, and proudly looking 'to traditional wisdoms'.[7] One commentator notes that Masdar City in Abu Dhabi is 'not an urban center but a sustainable village (that) employs low-cost, environmentally sound technologies … to sustain what is essentially village life'.[8] Ostensibly, these comments signal an urban regression, not an urban renaissance. Development, progress and mobility are meant to sweep away the reliance on custom, tradition and the rootedness to 'place'.

Unfortunately, Richard Florida hopes that such an infatuation with local simplicity will increasingly exert a 'powerful influence' over 'our "mating markets" and our ability to lead happy and fulfilled lives'.[9] The consequential dissolution of cities into localisms – urban villages, sustainable communities, insular neighbourhoods, Big Lunches and small changes – is a parochial slap in the face to the metropolitan mindset needed to maintain the ambition of urban life as a dynamic going concern.

London is now a hotbed of insular communities, paranoid environmentalists, anti-mobility advocates, conservation activists, defensive developers, austerity counsellors, navel-gazing psycho-geographers and urban memory consultants; all looking for certainty, but paradoxically merely reinforcing the concept of risk aversion and limits to growth.[10]

It is all a far cry from Madox Ford's celebration of uncertainty and life without boundaries. 'England,' he said, 'is a small country. The world is infinitesimal amongst the planets. But London is illimitable.'[11] If only we had such confidence today, what cities we could build. ⌂

ZEDfactory, BedZed, Wallington, 2002
Today, the Walking City refers to a city in which one is forced to walk.

Notes
1. Lewis Mumford, 'What Is a City?', *Architectural Record*, LXXXII, November 1937, p 94.
2. Ford Madox Ford, *The Soul of London: A Survey of a Modern City*, Everyman (London), 1995, p 111.
3. John Punter, *Urban Design and the British Urban Renaissance*, Taylor & Francis (London), 2009, p 350.
4. Lewis Mumford, *The City in History: Its Origins, Its Transformations, and Its Prospects*, Harcourt, Brace & World (New York), 1961.
5. Alan Weisman, *The World Without Us*, Virgin Books (London), 2008, p 98.
6. CJ Lim and Ed Liu, *Smart-Cities and Eco-Warriors*, Routledge (Abingdon), 2010.
7. Ibid, p 26.
8. Geeta Pradhan and Rajesh K Pradhan, 'Hybrid Cities: A Basis for Hope', *The Bridge: Earth Systems Engineering* 31: 1, Spring 2001, p 22.
9. Richard Florida, *Who's Your City? How the Creative Economy is Making the Place Where You Live the Most Important Decision of Your Life*, Basic Books (Toronto), 2008.
10. L Owen Kirkpatrick and Michael Peter Smith, 'The Infrastructural Limits to Growth: Rethinking the Urban Growth Machine in Times of Fiscal Crisis', *International Journal of Urban and Regional Research*, Vol 35, No 3, May 2011, pp 477–503.
11. Ford Madox Ford, op cit, p 15.

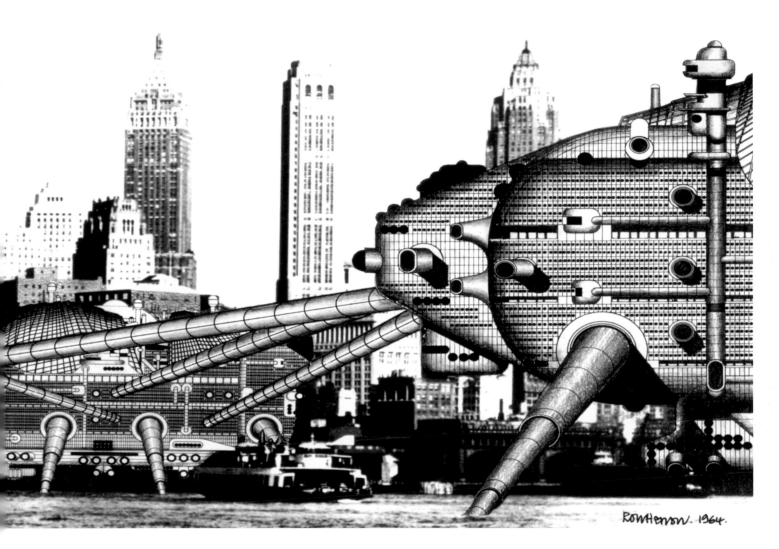

Ron Herron, *Walking City*, 1964
Here, the Walking City refers to an urban future in which the city walks for us.

A CITY?

David Littlefield

WHITE CITY

THE ART OF ERASURE AND FORGETTING THE OLYMPIC GAMES

Franco-British Exhibition of Science, Arts and Industry, White City, London, 1908
The Franco-British Exhibition ground. Aerial view over the White City exhibition ground,
taken from the Flip Flap amusement ride.

As London prepares to host the Olympic Games for the third time, **David Littlefield** reflects on the fortunes of White City, the West London site that hosted the event a little over a century ago.

On 4 April 1906, Mount Vesuvius erupted. A series of further eruptions that month were so energetic and disruptive, putting the Italian economy under so much strain, that Rome abandoned its intention to stage the 1908 Olympics. The International Olympic Committee later invited London to step in and host the event instead – just 20 months before the planned opening ceremony. To ease the burden, a number of events were held in pre-existing venues (tennis at Wimbledon, for example), but organisers quickly took advantage of plans to construct a vast new exhibition and entertainment complex on London's western fringe, adding a 93,000-capacity stadium to provide an impressive focus for the Games.

The White City stadium was the largest structure of its type in the world (it even included a swimming tank within the track enclosure), and the building signalled the beginning of the architectural spectacle that has become synonymous with the Olympics. Earlier games at Paris and St Louis (1900 and 1904 respectively) added the Games to pre-planned expositions, but did so in such an inclusive way that the sporting events appeared as sideshows. In Paris, the winner of the marathon had no idea he had been running in an Olympic event, and learned of his status 12 years later; track and field events took place in the Bois de Bologne and javelins often landed among trees; trees also, in fact, obscured views from the grandstand to the (sloping) running track. The St Louis event was better

Contemporary plan of the Franco-British Exhibition of Science, Arts and Industry, White City, London, 1908
The stadium, located mid-right, was the world's first purpose-built Olympic stadium. It was demolished in 1985.

Edward White, Drawings for the Franco-British Exhibition of Science, Arts and Industry, White City, London, 1908
Drawings by architect Edward White showing the assembly of techniques of the 1908 exhibition buildings. Plaster blocks were laid between steel stanchions.

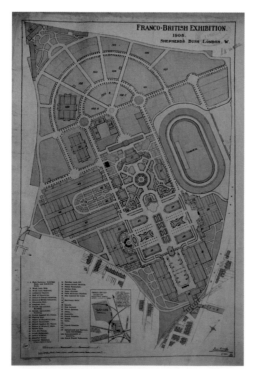

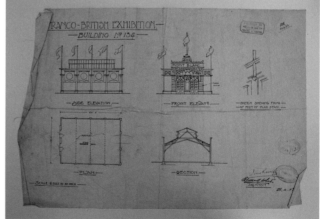

organised, but dragged on from May to November and included racially segregated events to contrive a sense of white superiority. 'Following hard on the heels of the 1900 debacle, St Louis 1904 threatened the continuance of the modern Olympics', write Gold and Gold.[1]

It would be some years before an Olympic Games would match the scale and splendour of London 1908, but one has to work very hard to find much evidence of the event now. The stadium was demolished in 1985, and the wider exhibition site (clad in white plaster, hence 'White City') has disappeared also. This pair of vast events and architectural enterprises has been the subject of such near obliteration that they reveal themselves through only the very faintest traces.

At the beginning of the 20th century, the land to the west and north of Shepherd's Bush comprised orchards, agricultural land, brick-making fields and rifle ranges. Wood Lane, running north to south, was little more than a track; the new housing of Notting Hill and Holland Park had been contained, momentarily, by the West London Railway line a little to the east; HM Prison Wormwood Scrubs, completed in 1891, stood in isolation. This zone could be described as an edge – not in the sense that Ford Madox Ford would have described it at the time ('nowadays we may say that London begins where tree trunks commence to be black),[2] but as a sudden drop in population density, a largely rural landscape where creeping urbanisation

has come into view. Good rail links and the inevitable westward expansion of London conspired to present this 57-hectare (140-acre) edge as the location for the Franco-British Exhibition of Science, Arts and Industry, held to celebrate the Entente Cordiale in 1908. Containing around 170 exhibition halls, kiosks, pavilions and other supporting structures, the site was laid out on a northwest/southeast axis around a series of waterways, formal gardens and a grid of thoroughfares. At the heart of it was the Elite Gardens, while further along the central diagonal route was the Flip Flap – a pair of giant counterbalanced arms that propelled joyriders 60 metres (197 feet) into the air. Eight million people visited the site between May and October 1908.

By the 1940s, much of the site had been covered by social housing, organised along a north–south/east–west grid that buries the curious diagonal of the exhibition site. Meanwhile, the stadium (which became something of a white elephant almost as soon as the Games ended) struggled on as a venue for greyhound racing, speedway, athletics and an occasional home for Queens Park Rangers Football Club. Contemporary maps list many of the buildings on the southern half of the site as 'ruins', and what had been open and largely agricultural land half a century earlier was already in need of regeneration. The steady erasure of the White City continued with the construction of BBC Television Centre and the subsequent demolition of the stadium and its recent replacement by the BBC Media Village that sits within its

---

Edward White, Elevation of the Daily Mail Pavilion, British-Franco Exhibition, White City, London, 1908
One of approximately 170 structures to occupy the 1908 White City exhibition site.

Edward White, Proposal for a footbridge over Wood Lane, White City, London, c 1908
The buildings and other structures which covered the White City site tended to deploy one of a small number of architectural languages: Beaux Arts, oriental or a local vernacular (such as Scottish castle or Tudor cottage).

The Flip Flap at the Franco British Exhibition, White City, London, 1908
Contemporary photograph of the Flip Flap, a fairground ride that propelled people 60 metres (197 feet) into the air. The site is now occupied by social housing.

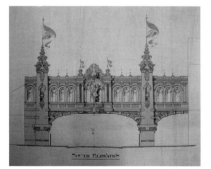

footprint. Evidence for the original White City is more or less restricted to place names and the pattern of a handful of roads that mark the position of exhibition routes. The overall name of the estate persists, despite the absence of any whiteness. 'How curious it is that places change so, and yet keep their old names!', observes the guide in William Morris' *News From Nowhere*.[3]

The names of newer streets, meanwhile, reflect their proximity to the location of former exhibition pavilions: Australia Road; New Zealand Way; Canada Way. South Africa Road, one of just two diagonal routes through today's site, follows the line of the original Palace Avenue. The other diagonal route follows the line described by the western edge of the stadium; originally called Stadium Avenue and renamed White City Road by the 1930s, this route has since been re-renamed Dorando Close. The origins of this later incarnation are less obvious than the memorials to exhibition sheds and colonial outposts. Dorando Pietri was first to complete the marathon in 1908 but, because the exhausted Italian was helped over the line by officials, he was disqualified and the American Johnny Hayes was declared the winner; Queen Alexandra, aware that the marathon had been extended from 25 miles to 26 miles and 385 yards in order that the race could start outside Windsor Castle and end in front of the stadium's royal box, later awarded Pietri a gold cup.

Walking the 57-hectare (140-acre) site today, it is striking how effectively its early urban history is buried. Its edges can still be traced against predevelopment boundary lines, and the local authority has recreated a Japanese garden on the site of an original dating from the Japan-British Exhibition of 1910. Further, the BBC has tacked the 1908 medal table to the facade of one of its Media Village buildings. But this is paltry stuff. Phipps House, one of many large social housing blocks that began to overlay the estate in the 1930s, is arranged around a quiet lawn, once the fulcrum for the Flip Flap; Television Centre sits astride the site of a boating lake; Canberra Primary School locates itself atop the bandstand, once the epicentre of a formal garden. Apart from an overlay of maps, there is no evidence for these observations.

If one were to consider a site as a document, most spaces that have been the subject of change would appear as a crowded text stuffed with marginalia, annotations, corrections, explanatory notes and rubbings out. These spaces, as documents, would be complex indeed: dense; perhaps difficult to read; and fantastically open to interpretation. White City is not so rich a document; it is an almost complete palimpsest, in that it is very nearly a total erasure and the subject of a rewriting. Moreover, as the condition of the physical profoundly shifts, so too does its ability to encapsulate memory.

Wembley, another example of event-led development on the city's periphery, is managing to leave a longer-lasting imprint. Developed as a further incarnation of the general mania for

---

The site for White City, 1896
Marked by orchards and brick fields, the site was little over a decade from being comprehensively developed as an exhibition and sporting venue.

White City, 1915
The Franco-British Exhibition of Science, Arts and Industry exhibition venue, complete with stadium, now occupies what had recently been a semi-rural edge zone.

White City, 1955
The exhibition site has begun to disappear under social housing. Buildings to the south of the site are marked as ruins. The BBC would later occupy much of the zone that had fallen into disrepair, covering the disused boating lake.

Olympic Games, White City, London, 1908
opposite bottom left: Dorando Pietri, the Italian winner of the 1908 Olympic marathon, was disqualified after collapsing and being helped over the line by officials.

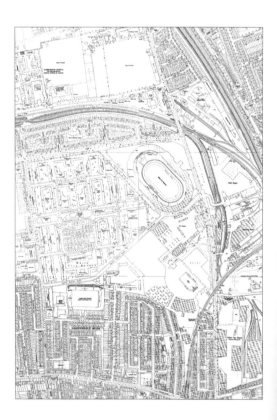

public festival and spectacle that characterised Edwardian London, the British Empire Exhibition of the mid-1920s occupied a site that was even more rural than White City at the turn of the century. Broadly contained within a triangular zone marked out by two railways and a road, the exhibition was set out on a similarly grandiose grid, with the stadium and the Palaces of Culture and Industry separated by formal boulevards and gardens. In fact, the Olympic Way roughly follows a route through Wembley Park that had become established by the 1890s; the circulation node at the centre of the park became preserved (and hugely inflated) in the British Empire Exhibition plan, bisecting it east–west and north–south. That plan persists today. The 'palaces' are no longer present, gardens have become car parks and the stadium has been entirely replaced, but there is sufficiently recognisable urban form to preserve the geologies of history and enhance cultural memories – indeed, mythologies. 'The new stadium at Wembley, home to the FA Cup Final from 1923, set the seal less on London's place in the game than on the place of the game in the nation's culture.'[4] The fact that it was Wembley, not White City, which hosted the 'austerity Olympics' in 1948 further enhances the site's status in the national consciousness.

White City rewrote the site on which it was constructed; it, in turn, has been erased and rewritten. This sequence of transformation provides it with, perhaps, the potential for

reimagining for which Wembley has no need – the combination of banality, loss and social/cultural richness sought by psychogeographers. 'Contemporary British psychogeography may be viewed as a creative space in which feelings of loss and redemption are explored and negotiated,' writes Alastair Bonnett. 'This body of work explores and re-imagines the forgotten nooks and crannies of ordinary landscapes. It seeks to re-enchant and re-mythologize prosaic geographies.'[5]

White City, a place of forgetfulness, might well benefit from a certain enchantment; Wembley, already a place of (hyperbolic) memory and the monumental, needs no further assistance in this regard. The Olympics, having arrived and disappeared from view in London's west, is now moving (via the city's north) eastwards. If the organisers' ambitions for the benefits that will accrue from the London 2012 Olympic and Paralympic Games are truly realised, the Stratford Games will almost inevitably succumb to physical erasure; the 17-day sporting event will have provided land more fit for economic purpose, to become occupied after the event by housing, commercial enterprises and parkland. We know this not just because of the planned 'legacy phase', but because the lesson is already there in White City. ∆

Hammersmith Park Japanese Garden, White City, London, 2011
top left: 1908/10, legacy – the Japanese garden. The Japan-British Exhibition of 1910 was one of a small number of further international events that used the White City site after its 1908 inauguration. The London Borough of Hammersmith and Fulham has recreated the Japanese garden from this period.

Wembley in the 1890s
right: The British Empire Exhibition of the 1920s located a stadium and exhibition halls on what had already been marked out as Wembley Park.

Notes
1, John R Gold and Margaret M Gold (eds), *Olympic Cities*, Routledge (London), 2011.
2. F Madox Ford, *The Soul of London: A Survey of a Modern City*, Chiswick Press (London), 1905.
3. W Morris, *News From Nowhere*, Project Guttenberg, 2007, p 35. See www.gutenburg.org.
4. J White, *London in the 20th Century*, Vintage (London), 2008.
5. A Bonnett, 'The Dilemmas of Radical Nostalgia in British Psychogeography', *Theory Culture Society* 26, 45, 2009.

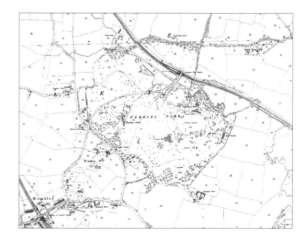

WHITE CITY, A PLACE OF FORGETFULNESS, MIGHT WELL BENEFIT FROM A CERTAIN ENCHANTMENT; WEMBLEY, ALREADY A PLACE OF (HYPERBOLIC) MEMORY AND THE MONUMENTAL, NEEDS NO FURTHER ASSISTANCE IN THIS REGARD.

Wembley in the 1930s
The urban grain of the British Empire Exhibition and sporting development survives nearly a century after it was conceived.

Robert Harbison

Weston Williamson, Dalston Junction
Station, Dalston, London, 2010
below: The new railway connection is
catalysing further development in terms of
both new building and reuse.

A NEW OVERGROUND LINE AND THE SENSE OF PLACE

Robert Harbison describes how the upgrading and extension of the old East London Line, which connects the city east and south, enables new explorations and insights.

There is a long tradition of seeing East London as remote and exotic. Victorian travellers were shocked at what they found there, which they conveyed by titles like *In Darkest England and the Way Out* (1890).[1] The whole idea of looking for remoteness near at hand will seem perverse to some readers, but it answers a deep human need. All travel is a search for the unfamiliar, and there is a special satisfaction in finding that you do not need to change your position much, just your way of looking, to encounter bottomless strangeness all around you.

Still, there is extra pleasure in making your journeys literal, boarding a train, arriving at a destination, wearing yourself out sampling a new place and then figuring out how to get home again. For residents to become travellers in their own cities they must behave differently, misusing familiar transport to make journeys that are not really necessary.

The new Overground line from Dalston to West Croydon creates new fault lines and constitutes a new urban geology by connecting places no one has thought of joining up before. For me almost all of it is real *terra incognita* and the very idea of being able to get easily from Dalston to Rotherhithe passing through Shoreditch and Wapping on the way suggests a whole new London at a stroke. You could

say that you are letting the train line dictate your experience of the city, but it is no more dictatorial than having someone suggest books for you to read.

There is too much of London to explore every bit of it. You need a principle of selection, and what better way of choosing this than to use stations on a line as nodes to fan out from and return to, in taking random samples in depth of the variety of the metropolis. There is always the question of whether anything as vast and confusing as London can really be perceived as one thing, but whatever the final answer, something makes you keep trying, by continually stretching the idea of what can be included and thus reframing the question.

For this observer, South London was even more dauntingly unknown than East, so much so that I had given up on any attempt to know it. One thing missing was a starting place, and the Overground solved this neatly, providing several: Rotherhithe, New Cross and, most outlandishly, Brockley. In some sense it must be getting it the wrong way round to think that the rail line brings the city into being, giving it intelligible structure, making sense of its tumult. But for an observer that is how it can appear, and the string of station names is the first reassuring sign of a solid backbone beneath the chaotic surface.

So the line brings the city into existence, or makes it possible to see it as more than a disconnected series of sensations. You do not need to fear that it will make things too rigid: there is still plenty of room for accident to play its part. When we did our expeditions there was still no smooth connection at Dalston and you had to make an awkward splice, walking between Dalston Junction and Dalston Central. This remained a hitch in the stride of all journeys even after we had the route down pat.

There is a feature here you could not miss, as long as you came in daylight and were heading east, but I still count it an accident because we were not expecting it and Dalston was not a stop, just a connection. It is a huge and lurid mural commemorating a peace march that must have passed down this road 30 years earlier. The artist who conceived it died before it was finished. We were only seeing it because of the incomplete state of the line, and it would

Mural, Dalston, London, 1985
opposite bottom: Designed by Ray Walker
and painted by Mike Jones and Anna
Walker, this commemoration of a peace
march seems unlikely to survive further
regeneration for much longer.

**JSA Architecture, Shoreditch High Street
Station, Shoreditch, 2010**
below: The new Overground station
provides a stark contrast to the gritty
existing railway arches and high street.

20

NUMBER OF BOROUGHS
THROUGH WHICH
THE LONDON OVER-
GROUND TRAVELS

The old East London Line has been extended, upgraded and linked into a wider network, creating strong connections for the first time between Highbury, Dalston and West Croydon. The London Overground is a network of suburban trains that travels through 20 of London's 33 boroughs. Largely completed by 2011 (but continuing into late 2012), the service incorporates the East London Line, which once ran a north–south shuttle between Shoreditch and New Cross. A £1 billion project to upgrade and integrate this line into a wider overground network began in 2005, and it will eventually form part of an orbital railway around the capital.

Phase 1 of the two-phase project was managed by Transport for London (TfL) and partly funded by the European Investment Bank as a regeneration package. Four new stations were built at Dalston Junction, Haggerston, Hoxton and Shoreditch High Street, while a northwards extension to Highbury & Islington (well served by the Underground network) has embedded it into the city's Tube service. The hope is that the line will trigger development in some of London's poorest boroughs.

A £1 BILLION PROJECT TO UPGRADE AND INTEGRATE THIS LINE INTO A WIDER OVERGROUND NETWORK BEGAN IN 2005

Cities are undeniably the solidest human products, yet looked at in detail they are among the most impermanent.

not be there for ever: it decorated the chopped-off end of a crumbling terrace. A little further along, a beautifully pompous and semi-derelict pub had become a betting shop, while all around were signs of demolition and rebuilding provoked by the new rail line. In a year's time this would all look different.

What does the student of London do about the landmarks that are not there any more or the parts that are disappearing before his eyes? Give up, resign himself, savour them all the more because they will not last? Cities are undeniably the solidest human products, yet looked at in detail they are among the most impermanent. Sometimes, when taking students around a district I know relatively well I am pulled up short by how much time I spend describing what is not there. In the 1970s when I was new in London I spent a fair while at intervals looking for Columbia Market, a Victorian behemoth that got a striking full-page picture in one of Nikolaus Pevsner's London volumes. It was further east than I had any other reason to go, so I was unsure of my bearings, but did not give up searching. I never found it, and only came across a printed reference to its demolition years later. It was a magnificent structure (lots of images now on various websites), but it had outlived its usefulness practically as soon as it was built, so one wonders how it lasted so long – into the 1960s – rather than how it disappeared.

Now I stand on the concrete roof of the underground garage that fills most of the site, looking at the bleak 1960s council flats that surround it, perhaps a piazza in the mind of its designer, and feel that the space is still enriched by the earlier, equally misguided attempt at creating new kinds of urban space.

Near the bottom end of the Isle of Dogs, the most altered region in all of London, there used to be a fantastic gnome garden with hundreds of plaster creatures arranged on shelves to form an outdoor museum. One day I passed and the shelves were empty. The owner was circling forlornly in the little space behind the hedge; his treasures had been taken in the night and he was ready to pack it in once and for all.

I do not know if he moved away. I do not even know exactly where his garden was, but I always look for it when I am there, and now orient myself by the iron skeleton of a factory nearby. That too has been marked for ages as the projected site of luxury dwellings and has covered its hoardings with enticing pictures of parties the residents will have.

I started out meaning to write about what London is becoming, and have gravitated to what it is no longer. But these are points on a continuum: exploring the city one is continually aware of how completely it expresses itself in change. Buildings sometimes last, but almost inevitably their surroundings and their uses change. It often seems that looking for specific bits of architecture in a city is like looking for needles in haystacks. You can easily miss some of the best buildings. Others are not where they were meant to be: the world has moved on and left them stranded. I am thinking particularly of Thomas Archer's magnificent early 18th-century church in Deptford. Or they are so defaced by decades of raucous misuse, like Shoreditch High Street just across from the old parish church, that it takes a Sherlock Holmes of architectural styles to detect them under various overlays. Or they have deliberately planted themselves in an unlikely place, like an inspiring piece of recent architecture, Herzog

Exploring the city one is continually aware of how completely it expresses itself in change.

& de Meuron's Laban school of dance beside Deptford Creek.

Spurred into action by the overground, or in the first place by the map that sketched possible journeys, I have come to some new ideas about the structure or the nature of the city. But they are not new; you can find them in Modernist art or in the films of Marc Isaacs. These are structures that look at first like pure randomness. They have the freedom of the random, against which the consistency of the interpreter's vision increasingly asserts itself. So finally you feel that the film-maker, or you the explorer, have let the world be itself, but that out of this seeming passivity real illumination has come. △

Note
1. William Booth, *In Darkest England and the Way Out*, Salvation Army (London), 1890.

Rafael Viñoly, Battersea Power Station Masterplan, Battersea,
London, due for completion 2024
top and right: The public space in front of Battersea Power Station
includes a 300-metre (984-foot) stretch of river frontage, a new
ferry wharf and 2.4 hectares (6 acres) of landscaped parkland.

Edward Denison

BATTERSEA / NINE ELMS

above right: Artist's impression of one of the turbine halls in the regenerated Battersea Power Station, which will house a mixture of commercial, office and semi-industrial uses.

Sir Giles Gilbert Scott, Battersea Power Station, London, 1933/1953
top: The site of the proposed development by Real Estate Opportunities who commissioned the masterplan by Rafael Viñoly.

Rafael Viñoly, Battersea Power Station Masterplan, Battersea, London, due for completion 2024
above: Artist's impression of Battersea Power Station's regeneration when completed.

KieranTimberlake, New US Embassy, Nine Elms, London, due for completion 2017
Artist's impression of the new US Embassy at Nine Elms, designed by KieranTimberlake.

The forlorn carcass of Battersea's once-majestic power station on the south bank of the Thames marks the site of London's largest regeneration project. The four iconic and classically dressed chimney stacks ceased belching when the Modernist monument formed by the sublime marriage of two independent power stations (built in 1933 and 1953) was decommissioned in 1983. For 30 years the four columns of this 'temple of power', styled by Sir Giles Gilbert Scott, whose creative hand bestowed London with Bankside Power Station (now Tate Modern) and furnished Britain with the classic red K2 telephone box, towered over southwest London. For the past 20 years the building, along with the long stretch of prime river frontage it dominates, has stood neglected, scarring the face of London for too long. After many false starts, the site is ripe for regeneration. In 2008, the owner, Real Estate Opportunities (majority owned by Treasury Holdings), commissioned the architect Rafael Viñoly to draft a masterplan that is intended to rejuvenate the power station site and to stimulate the regeneration of the adjacent Nine Elms Corridor extending to Vauxhall. The combined sites represent the largest Opportunity Area in the Mayor of London's London Plan. Estimated at £5.5 billion and expected to be completed

by 2024, Viñoly's masterplan comprises 743,224 square metres (8 million square feet) of space catering for residential, office, retail, hotel, leisure and cultural uses. Phase one will be designed by Ian Simpson Architects and de Rijke Marsh Morgan (dRMM) and consists of two mixed-use buildings situated to the west of the power station containing homes, offices, studios, restaurants and shops in over 92,903 square metres (1 million square feet) of space. Construction is expected to start in mid-2012 and be completed in 2016.

Sixteen new buildings will be erected around three sides of the power station; none will be higher than the base of the chimneys at 60 metres (197 feet). Ranging from 8 to 18 storeys high, the terraced profiles of these buildings will create almost 5.3 hectares (13 acres) of rooftop gardens. In addition, 2.4 hectares (6 acres) of landscaped open space along the 300-metre (984-foot) long river frontage will safeguard the views of the power station from the north and across the river. The whole project is expected to create 3,400 homes and a quarter of a million square metres (2.7 million square feet) of office and commercial space, and generate over 20,000 construction jobs and 15,000 long-term jobs.

2024 EXPECTED COMPLETION DATE FOR RAFAEL VIÑOLY'S MASTERPLAN

Battersea and Nine Elms Opportunity Area
Aerial view of the entire site including the new US Embassy by KieranTimberlake and the New Covent Garden site by Foster + Partners and Neil Tomlinson Architects. The area will be served by an extension of the Northern Line and two new Tube stations at Nine Elms and Battersea.

Rafael Viñoly, Battersea Power Station Masterplan, Battersea, London, due for completion 2024
Aerial view of the proposed development of the Battersea Power Station site.

The regeneration of the power station is a central facet of the ecologically inspired masterplan, generating power for the site from renewable resources as well as being a heating and cooling plant – making it the largest zero-carbon building in Britain and possibly even the world. It will also house a museum, exhibition spaces and offices.

On the adjacent Nine Elms Corridor site will be a revamped New Covent Garden Market designed by Foster + Partners and Neil Tomlinson Architects, and a new US Embassy by KieranTimberlake. Following the US government's decision to uproot from its 50-year-old Mayfair home designed by Eero Saarinen, the embassy chose Nine Elms for its proximity to Central London and riverside access. In 2010, American architects KieranTimberlake won the commission to design the new embassy. Construction will begin in 2013 and is expected to be finished in 2017.

Although the building's environmental credentials appealed to the client, it is hard not to see this isolated glass cube as anything other than a modern-day keep with ominous comparisons to the Tower of London further downstream. The US Embassy optimistically claims the building is 'a beacon that is a respectful icon representing the strength of the US–

UK relationship', but the most conspicuous relationship that this modern tower, surrounded by landscaped gardens and a miniature lake, has with Britain is its historic connection to the myriad defensive structures that litter the landscape, recalling countless attempts to build security: medieval fortified manors and moats, Norman keeps and castles, Anglo-Saxon burhs and earthworks, Iron Age hill forts.

Linking the Nine Elms and Battersea sites with the rest of London will be a new riverboat service and an extension of the Northern Line from Kennington. The two new stations, Nine Elms and Battersea, costing somewhere between £550 million and £660 million, will be the first privately funded stations on London's Underground network and are expected to be opened in 2017. ⌂

Terry Farrell & Partners, Location Map of the Great Estates and Large-Scale Single Landowners, 2007
Following growth in population and the continuing expansion outwards of the metropolis, the estates became the cultivated urbanism of well-to-do London – completing the transition from agriculture to 'urbiculture'.

Large Single Landownerships
in 19th C and today

The City Of London
The Portman Estate
The Cadogan Estate
The Grosvenor Estate
Fitzrovia
Bloomsbury
Great Estates
Borough Boundaries

Terry Farrell

THE ROLE OF THE ESTATES

FROM AGRICULTURE TO URBICULTURE

Large swathes of London's West End remain under the ownership of the Great Estates, with the Grosvenor Estate (Duke of Westminster) owning much of Mayfair and the Cadogan family (Earl of Cadogan) much of Chelsea. **Terry Farrell** looks at how this long-term custodianship has impacted on the development of the fabric of the city and its strong sense of place. He explains how it is a model that he has tried to draw from in his own Earl's Court masterplan.

Evolution, not revolution, is often stated as being the British way of change: piecemeal, progressive and not cohering to an overarching plan. London, in its assembly of towns and villages into an urban conglomerate, has grown and continues to grow, in this way. A collection of complementary interests, capital investments and the physical shaping force of topography have seen a shift in land use and development over the centuries, from agricultural land to a set of urban estates owned and managed by families and organisations with vested interests in the careful, considered and intelligent use of this most scarce of resources.

The oldest of the Great Estates, as they are collectively known, were once agricultural landholders, occupying the land between the royal estates of the Regent's Park to the north and St James's Park to the south. At Marylebone, the Howard de Walden Estate – which manages the high street and surrounding land – follows a pattern of settlement established in the medieval period. The river Tyburn, originating in Hampstead, formed the focal point for a series of small villages to develop along its banks, between the royal hunting grounds of Regent's Park and St James's. Adjacent to these settlements, on the lands to the west and east, between riverbeds, grew farm holdings that were to eventually gain a geometric field pattern and form the basis for 18th- and 19th-century estates to grow and develop into what we see today. Gradually, and in an evolutionary manner, following growth in population and the continuing expansion outwards of the metropolis, these estates became the cultivated urbanism of well-to-do London – completing the transition from agriculture to 'urbiculture'. Today, Marylebone High Road is still shaped by the Tyburn, hidden beneath its length in a deep culvert that, apocryphally, emerges through the basement of an antiques shop along the road.

The large estates of Central London mostly followed this model of development, with inhabitation along London's tributaries gradually growing into established settlements. And here, within this model of long-term ownership, is an approach to the creation and management of city space based around an enlightened form of urban stewardship. Estates such as the Howard de Walden at Marylebone, the Portman, Cadogan and Grosvenor all follow similar patterns of development, but most importantly they share the same approach to a carefully developed land-holding that places the quality of the urban realm at the very fore. As custodians of the land for perpetuity, the estates can take a long-term and large-scale view of the development of their built environment. This is a very British approach to land-holding and we have seen extraordinary examples of its application overseas. As a colonial power, Britain imposed such a model on Hong Kong which led to the growth of one of the world's most successful economies. The Chinese have understood its value and assimilated it, making the Hong Kong model an internationally recognised way of providing exemplary urban stewardship over many decades. This model is different to that of the contemporary public sector in the UK which struggles with planning proactively in the same way. In today's economic climate, local authorities tend to see their land-holdings as assets to reduce fiscal debt and not for long-term value creation.

The estates do not function outside of the economics of our time, of course. Through an enlightened approach to working with the public sector in planning the future use of the land, the harsh realities of austerity can be mitigated by a long-term vision of an urban future. Currently in London we are seeing the continued growth of the estates model, not least of which can be seen in the progressive rejuvenation of previously overlooked

---

Terry Farrell & Partners, The lost rivers of London and the historic districts of London that grew alongside them, 2010
Like the estates of west-central London, the land along the banks of, for example, the lost river 'Counters Creek' has made the progression from agriculture to urbiculture and, through urban stewardship, is being brought back as an established place in the city.

Cover of Sir Terry Farrell's Book, *Shaping London: The Patterns and Forms that Make the Metropolis,* **2010**

The imaginary Time Out guide for Earls Court in the year 2030, commissioned by Capital & Counties, is an example of a landowner consulting in an innovative and proactive way on the future of their development.

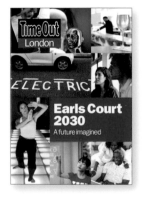

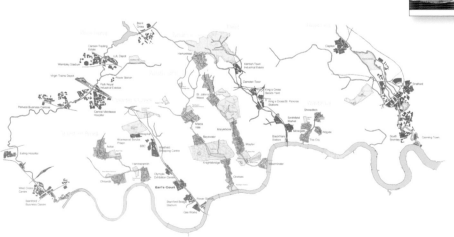

areas of the capital. At Earl's Court, for example, investment and development company Capital and Counties Properties has worked closely with local communities to understand the current cultural and economic value of the area. This is a place with a thriving, but somewhat unknown, creative centre, a strong Australasian community and a successful business district; it needs careful consideration of its development potential over a long time period, which has been central to the engagement with local communities and stakeholders. Activities such as the imaginary *Time Out* guide to Earl's Court in the year 2030 and the myearlscourt.com website, which has been visited by over 25,000 people, are exemplary ways of engaging in a meaningful way. By taking a proactive and long-term look at what an area could be like 20 years into the future, Capital and Counties has been able to consider its role as urban custodians, as well as developers, in creating a place that will remain successful and thriving through the challenges that London will face in the next two or three decades.

The advantages of this model of landownership are clear to see: an estate with interests in the economic return of an area, half a century or more down the line, takes decisions and produces plans that create places, not just buildings. At Earl's Court, the provision of housing, workplaces, and leisure, creative and community facilities have been central to the long-term success of this most recent of estates. By creating four villages with quite unique characters and carefully considered parks and squares, while providing up to 8,000 new homes, a similar process of stewardship of the urban realm is at work here as in the established estates of the 18th and 19th centuries. Place is created first and foremost, which gives a defined heart to a community, around which is gathered the workplaces, shops and

Earl's Court model photo showing Farrells' proposed masterplan.

Farrells' vision for Earl's Court – 'Four Villages and a High Street'.

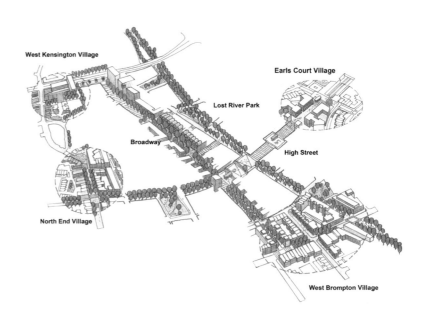

West Kensington Village

Earls Court Village

Lost River Park

Broadway

High Street

North End Village

West Brompton Village

Terry Farrell & Partners, Regent's Place, London, 2010
Farrells' masterplan for Regent's Place in the West End of London.

homes that make a community flourish. By thinking decades into the future, and providing for social changes, Capital and Counties is working to make a place that is a home for both residents and businesses for years, not only in the short term. Like the estates of west-central London, this land along the banks of the lost river 'Counters Creek' has made the progression from agriculture to urbiculture and, through urban stewardship, is being brought back as an established place in the city. Rather than trying to build a place in and of itself, the masterplan Farrells has created seeks to draw on the styles and typologies of existing communities, and integrate them; through this approach their potential can be developed, ensuring that the masterplan remains sympathetic to the local area.

Stewardship requires an understanding of the context that one's land sits in, and an understanding of the position of that

10,000

NUMBER OF WORKERS EACH
WEEK IN REGENT'S PLACE,
A CUT-OFF AREA NOW
RETURNED TO ACTIVE AND
VIBRANT USE

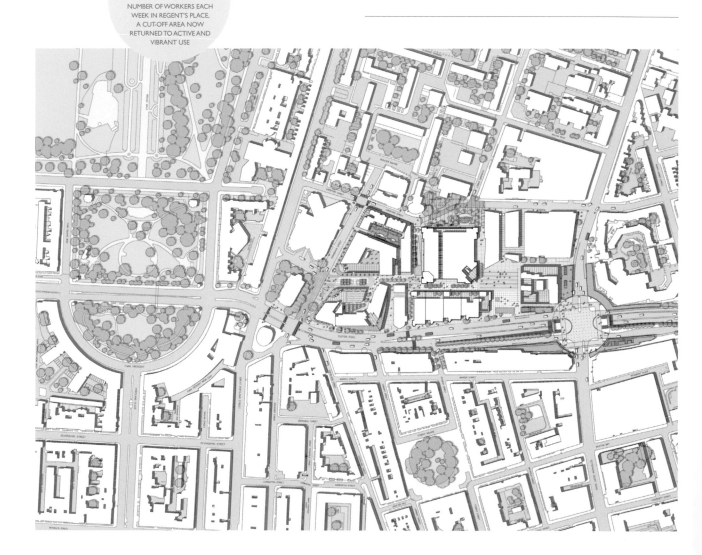

At Regent's Place in the West End, British Land has guided the development of this section of London for 25 years, and has a long-term commitment to the continued success of this location as a newly emerging place for work, leisure and trade.

place within the overall fabric of the city. At Regent's Place in the West End, British Land has guided the development of this section of London for 25 years, and has a long-term commitment to the continued success of this location as a newly emerging place for work, leisure and trade. The work of British Land has seen a previously cut-off section of Central London, home to over 10,000 workers during the week, returned to active and vibrant use. It is positioned to the north of the Euston Road and adjacent to Regents Park, and Farrells' work in advising and establishing an understanding of the situation of the land in historical and contemporary contexts has been key to its current success. Through analysing the relationship of the area to the adjacent West End and Fitzrovia, and careful consideration of the failures in the past to manage pedestrian and traffic flows at the Euston Circus junction with Tottenham Court Road, British Land has been able to influence and stimulate the growth of a new urban place. Large landowners, through their long-term commitment to the establishment of high-value real estate, are recognised as leading contributors to the sustainable urban development of the capital. Organisations such as British Land have won awards for built environment and biodiversity from champions of such causes as the *Guardian* newspaper, and provide excellent examples of how to holistically incorporate the very real agendas of the future into successful business models of land stewardship. Farrells' engagement comes from an approach to the city that sees the organisation of London as based on a pattern of emergent, contextually led planning, as opposed to object-led design. As at Marylebone, where the high street is held up as one of Britain's finest, certainly in terms of its urban qualities and extraordinary mix of uses, so the establishment of high-quality places is key in

contemporary manifestations of a traditional form.

From the first Great Estates of the Crown, through the agricultural-to-urbicultural estates of Howard de Walden, Portman, Grosvenor and others, to the new estates of corporate landowners, a historical continuity exists in the shaping of London through these enlightened custodians of our urban realm. The careful cultivation from an agricultural asset, where crops were planted and nurtured, to an urban one where houses, offices, churches, pubs and all manner of buildings have been sown, cared for and managed over long periods of time, has bequeathed London a unique and internationally significant model for growing our cities. These active, vibrant and dense neighbourhoods are essentially place-based developments whose long-termism is central to their success, and can provide a way to renurture overlooked and underused areas of the capital. As is being seen at King's Cross with the developers Argent, through constructing human-scale places significant organisations can be attracted to settle an area, drawing in associated residents, culture and business. But these require an investment that is long term, committed and able to see the emergence of value, in both assets and cultural capital, decades down the line. The Great Estates of London have proven the benefit of investing in an urban future, and have shaped the capital in a unique and exemplary manner. The challenge for the future of London is to ensure local authorities and other landowners adopt the same approach to the stewardship of the city's urban realm. ⌂

Text © 2012 John Wiley & Sons Ltd. Images: pp 86–7, 88(l), 89(r), 90 © Terry Farrell & Partners ltd; p 88(c) © 2010 John Wiley & Sons Ltd; p 88(r) © Time Out Group Ltd 2011; p 89(l) © Terry Farrell & Partners ltd. Photo: Andrew Putler; p © Terry Farrell & Partners ltd. Photos Andrew Haslam

Farrells' commercial buildings for 10 and 20 Tilton Street, Regent's Place.

Through far-sighted stewardship and investment in the public realm, British Land has been able to stimulate growth in a previously isolated section of Central London.

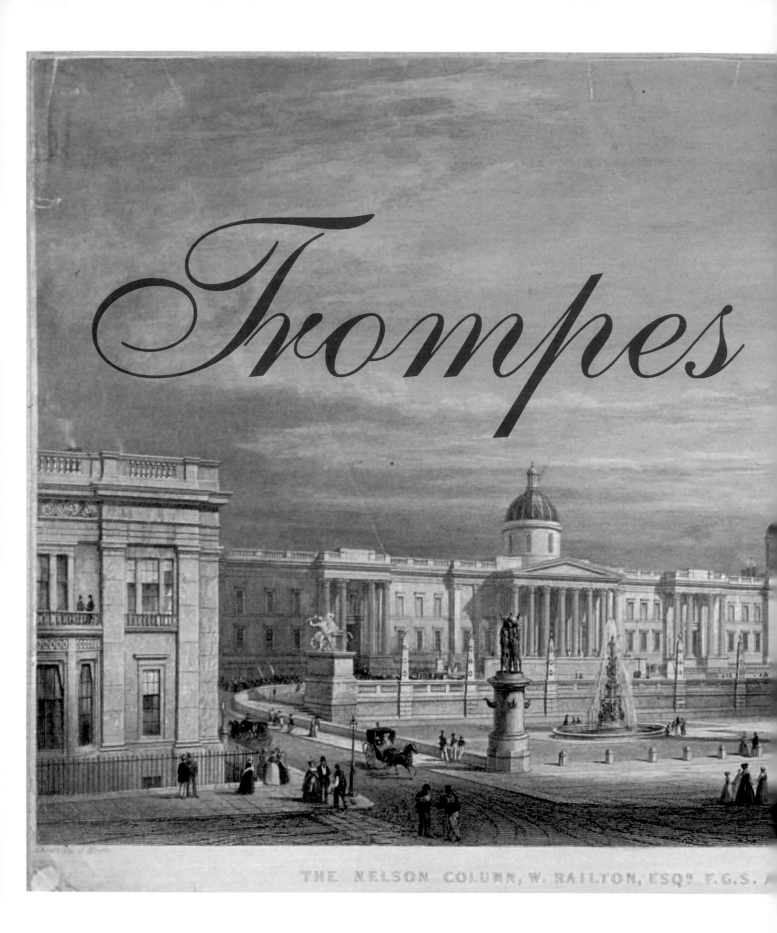

Trompes

THE NELSON COLUMN, W. RAILTON, ESQ⁵ F.G.S.

Mike Devereux

L'Oeil

ITECT, WITH THE IMPROVEMENTS OF TRAFALGAR SQUARE.

G Moore, Nelson's Column and the National Gallery in Trafalgar Square, London, 1842
Urban planning was used to turn London into the capital of an empire. It was later to be used to the same end by Napoléon III in Paris.

Mike Devereux sets out to explode the myth that London is an organic, unplanned city shaped by economic forces, and Paris is, in contrast, a planned city moulded by the state. He describes the many similarities that the two cities share and how planning ideas in fact 'flowed between the capitals' during the Haussmann era.

A Tale of Two Scales
top: The official mayoral boundary of Paris (green) superimposed on that of London (red)

Great James Street, London, 1960
above: Planned and built in accordance with the London Rebuilding Act 1667.

94

Received wisdom has it that London's urban history is one of slow evolution, while Paris is the subject of the strategic plan. However, the reality is much more fluid.

When, in 1733, Voltaire (1694–1778) praised the liberal commercial spirit of London and bemoaned the disdain with which Parisian aristocratic classes viewed such activity,[1] he set up a starkly contrasting way in which the two cities can be understood. This understanding has all too often been used to explain the cities' physical manifestations, eclipsing more complex interpretations. Extrapolating Voltaire's narrative of disparity has seen London portrayed as the organic, unplanned result of economic liberalism, driven by the goal of maintaining the city's global position. Further, it naively explains Paris as a 'planned' city *par excellence* – the result of a *dirigiste* state apparatus exercising control over two million Parisians living '*intra-muros*'. This impression was reinforced when the city wall was finally demolished in 1919–29 to make way for the Périphérique; this boundary still defines the physical and administrative edge of the city, alienating the nine million '*banlieusards*' living '*extra-muros*'. This hard London/Paris dichotomy can be challenged, however.

Beyond the uniform Parisian *calcaire* (limestone),[2] there is much similarity between the capitals. Both are Roman (Lutèce and Londinium). Their street patterns, from Petit Pont to rue St Jacques, and London Bridge to Bishopsgate, still reflect those Latinate beginnings. Terry Farrell sees London as a series of organic developments to which can be added royal palaces, government buildings and so on.[3] Much the same could be said of Paris, with Le Marais, St Germain, Abbesses, La Chapelle, Le Louvre, Palais des Tuileries and Palais de Luxembourg. Now joined by the pressures of a growing population into a capital city, but still with their own personalities,[4] both cities expanded as major ports with all the associated infrastructure that brought with it (indeed the symbol of the Mairie de Paris is still a ship), and both now celebrate modern riverfront regeneration.

When Napoléon III (1808–73) appointed Georges-Eugène, 1st Baron Haussmann (1809–91) as Préfet de la Seine in 1853 its organic foundation was imprinted on the city, and much of the grand architecture of the Paris we know today was already complete or underway. What makes his interventions in Paris significant is that Napoléon brought his experience of England to his philosophy of modern planning. London had experienced enormous developments in regulated city planning by the time he was exiled in England during the 1830s and 1840s. The Great Fire of 1666 and the Rebuilding Act of the following year, followed by the second Rebuilding Act of 1671, produced a hierarchy of streets and frontages (such as Great James Street, 1721), as well as Christopher Wren's (1632–1723) churches and the courage to build densely that gives the city its present morphology.

Building beyond the City boundaries was carefully planned, as were the estate developments of the West End such as Bloomsbury and the Grosvenor's Mayfair and Belgravia. All brought Parisian-like uniformity and harmony. There might not have been an overall 'city plan', and it was often aristocratic speculation via the leasehold system that imposed a broad grid and architectural style. But it was not a free-for-all. Each estate was linked to neighbouring development in much the same way as in that most 'planned' of cities – Bath. The result was pleasing and commercially efficient. By 1800, 30 West End squares had been laid out. Under the patronage and direction of the Prince Regent, John Nash (1752–1835) planned Regent's Park and Regent Street (1811–30) and Trafalgar Square (1820). All of which led Anthony Sutcliffe to remark that 'in these two, the West End had its Haussmann and its Napoléon half a century earlier'.[5]

Napoléon saw all this and more during his period of exile. He witnessed the economic and social impact of the Industrial Revolution, and he appreciated the value of good communications. In London, one of the first bypasses (Euston Road of 1756) and the capital's first railway stations (Euston, 1837, and Paddington, 1838) had been built. Napoléon understood the forces behind the transformation of London into a modern, commercial, working city and he took these lessons back to Paris in 1848. Crucially, he understood the need for 'modern' planning – an integrated approach to considering the urban fabric in which the city is perceived as a whole. Economic interests are served by creating and maintaining ideal conditions for business, while creating urban forms which are socially minded and aesthetically pleasing – what Karine Huguenaud calls 'l'urbanisme à vocation sociale'.[6]

In 1848, as many as 18,000 Parisians died of cholera,[7] prompting Napoléon to send a delegation to London to study workers' housing. He promoted the translation of Henry Roberts' book *The Dwellings of the Labouring Classes*[8] and gave aid to Paris' earliest social housing project, the Cité Napoléon. Constructed by the Société des Cités Ouvrières, the project was built around a courtyard with concierge, providing a model that could be repeated as slums were cleared and Paris expanded with the laying out of boulevards to link privately developed railway stations.

It is in the development of the Parisian parks that Napoléon III's social motives and English influence are best seen. Impressed by the parks and squares of London, he ordered Haussmann to create a *ville verte* (green city)[9] to mirror them – '*comme on le faisait à Londres*'.[10] Using the speculative approach that allowed the development of much of London, Bois de Boulogne (1852–8) and Parc Monceau (1861) were laid out in the west. In the east the Bois de Vincennes (1860) was provided for the city's workers; in the south Parc Montsouris (begun 1867) was deliberately planned for use by '*riches ou pauvres*'.[11] All were designed in the English tradition. Twenty-four squares were created to copy, as Haussmann's memoires put it, '*nos voisins d'outre-mer*'.[12] Such was their popularity that there are now 252 listed on the Mairie de Paris website.[13] Ideas on modern planning flowed between the capitals: the new drainage system in Paris was designed following extensive visits and research by Haussmann's engineer, Mille, into London's approach.

It is easy to forget that London, too, was being considered centrally and strategically. In 1855 Parliament passed the Metropolis Management Act and set up the Metropolitan Board of Works covering the area later designated as being under the control of the London County Council (1889). The board planned major developments such as the expanded drainage system (1865), the Embankments (1868–74) and major road construction in Central London, including Northumberland Avenue, Charing Cross Road and Shaftesbury Avenue. As in Paris, these projects involved slum clearance and made the capital

George Sidney Shepherd, Euston Station in Euston Square, London, c 1838
The arrival of the train brought the need for improved road access to the city centre from new stations.

METROPOLITAN TRAFFIC RELIEF

Thomas Shotter Boys, View of Regent Street looking towards what is now Piccadilly Circus, London, 1842
above centre: The grand urbanism of London came before the Grands Boulevards of Paris.

London Traffic Relief Scheme, c 1850
above: Even before Haussmann was appointed by Napoléon III in Paris, planning for London's growing population already included ideas for underground roads and services.

Plan for the proposed construction of Regent Street, London, 1818
Linking city to park by grand boulevard was a technique widely
employed afterwards in Paris.

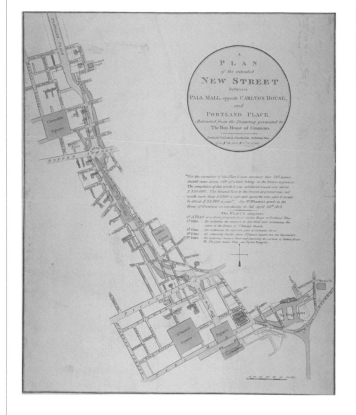

*Suburban
expansion in the
20th century
and the growth
of commuting
saw time
and space
compressed.*

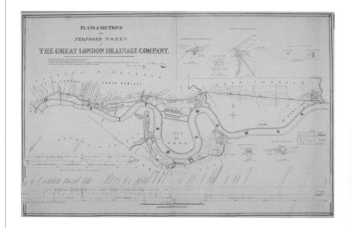

**JJ Morewood, Plan and section showing the proposed works of the
Great London Drainage Company, 1847**
above: Modernising London was a priority in order to cope with the
changing economic circumstances of the 19th century

fit for modern traffic. The board also purchased Hampstead Heath for public use.

Suburban expansion in the 20th century and the growth of commuting saw time and space compressed. Paris followed London with a metro that was (due to short-sighted and heavily political planning) constrained within its walls – and it still is. London emulated imperial Paris with the improved Mall and the installation of the Marble and Admiralty arches, while the redevelopment of Aldwych and Kingsway (1905) continued the Victorian road-improvement plan and cleared away much inner-city slum housing. While Paris was spared the destruction of the Second World War, London had to rebuild and, as if to dispel any myth of underplanning, the City generated a series of major visions: the County of London Plan (1943), Greater London Plan (1944), City of London Plan (1956) and the Greater London Development Plan (1969). These favoured dense commercial development within the City, while Paris, on the other hand, went outside to La Défense to develop its 'square mile'.

Both capitals underwent painful transformation in the 1960s – witness Les Halles and Euston Arch. The 1980s put an end to the working ports, encouraging an embrace of global capitalism. London led with St Katherine's Dock and Docklands, while Paris followed with Bercy Village and Rive Gauche. While the Grands Projets of Paris – the Centre Pompidou (1977), Musée d'Orsay (1986), La Pyramide du Louvre (1988), Bibliothèque Nationale (1996) and so on – might be seen as symbolic of a continuing *dirigiste* hand, London can boast as many: Covent Garden, the National Gallery's Sainsbury Wing (1991), the Jubilee Line extension (1999), the British Museum's Great Court (2000), Tate Modern (2000), the Millennium Bridge (2000, reopened 2002) … The tradition continues in both cities with an expensive rebuild of Les Halles and the rejuvenation of St Pancras. London's grand projects have been delivered, perhaps, in a typically British understated manner, without the pomp and ceremony of Parisian equivalents.

Paris is now examining how it might plan for inclusive expansion beyond the constraints of the Périphérique.[14] London's planning traditions have much to offer Paris by way of learning and example, just as it did to Napoléon III and Haussmann. London's experience of involving the private sector alongside public involvement, and its track record in *urbanisme*, strategic planning and governance, can all inform Paris. Celebrating planning achievements, which Paris does so well, is something that London should not be shy to do, in respect of both its past successes and present adventures. ∆

Notes
1. Voltaire, *Letters Concerning the English Nation*, Oxford University Press (Oxford), original 1733, reprint 1999. Originally published in English, translated into French as *Lettres Philosophiques* 1734.
2. The quarries of the Oise to the north of Paris supplied almost all the limestone – *calcaire* – used during Haussmann's reshaping of the city; until then Paris had been built using similar limestone from underneath the city itself.
3. Terry Farrell, *Shaping London: The Patterns and Forms That Make the Metropolis*, John Wiley & Sons (London), 2010.
4. Anthony Sutcliffe, *Autumn of Central Paris: Defeat of Town Planning 1850–1970*, Hodder & Stoughton (London), 1970.
5. Anthony Sutcliffe, *London: An Architectural History*, Yale University Press (New Haven, CT), 2006.
6. Karine Huguenaud, 1997; see www.napoleon.org/fr/magazine/itineraires/files/parcs-jardins.asp.
7. www.mapforum.com/15/blmap.htm.
8. Henry Roberts, *The Dwellings of the Labouring Classes: Society for Improving the Condition of the Labouring Classes*, London, 1851. See also www.ohio.edu/chastain/ip/pubhous.htm.
9. Patrice De Moncan, *Les Jardins d'Haussmann*, Les Editions du Mècène (Paris), 2009, p 9.
10. Georges Eugène Haussmann, *Mémoires du Baron Haussmann, Tome III*, Victor-Havard (Paris), 1893, p 240.
11. Ibid, p 240.
12. Ibid, p 239.
13. http://parcsetjardins.equipement.paris.fr/?tid=91.
14. Philippe Subra, *Le Grand Paris*, Armand Colin (Paris), 2009.

Aldwych from Kingsway, 1925
A Parisian boulevard in London.

THE PO OF THE

… the original is unfaithful to the translation
— Luis Borges[1]

(Re)generation has been driven by the exploitation of images: images produced by urban designers, architects and others to promote and sell speculative development. For designers today the scale of operation has expanded to new proportions: entire neighbourhoods and towns such as the Thames Gateway, Canary Wharf (and soon the Lea Valley) have been commodified through pre-emptive imagery. Contemporary designers have recently extended the modes and methods for manipulating and/or sublimating reality through advances in computer technology: multidisciplinary teams produce assemblage cityscapes from hybridised marketing strategies, sales brochures, glossy images, billboards, propaganda, text and multimedia. These images align technology, politics, communication, economics, journalism and society along with physical and natural worlds on to a two-dimensional plane (electronic or paper). Reality and fiction are barely discernible as they are substituted by imaginary histories and future archaeologies that coalesce until they reach critical mass as

'reality'. The regenerated city becomes a form of 'magical realism' – it is not pure fantasy; it is *real* – but one that has been extended through that which is mythological, phantasmal or ethereal.

The image here is an early representation, by Alejandro Zaera-Polo Architects/Foreign Office Architects, of the London 2012 Olympic and Paralympic Games project. Since the creation of the image, conditions have changed; only ever intended as a declaration of the ambition of the Games, not as a facsimile of a future building project, the context surrounding the vision has been shaken by global economic meltdown, ongoing financial uncertainty, political change and a strategic decision within the Olympic Delivery Authority (ODA) to focus on sustainability and reuse. Nonetheless, the dynamics of this early image are worth examination.

The Olympic bidding committee galvanised around this image as the centrefold for selling, branding and generating the Games. In order to do this, the image realises complex multiplicities. For example, it must communicate to the plurality of heterogeneous stakeholders: the London Organising Committee of the Olympic and Paralympic Games (LOCOG),

WER IMAGE

Designers have long used fantastical imagery as part of an urban regeneration process. Here, **Louis Rice** examines the legacy of Foreign Office Architects' seminal image for the 2005 winning bid for the London 2012 Olympic and Paralympic Games.

venture capitalists, the International Olympic Committee, the British public, local communities, central government, London's mayor, Sports England and many others. It is selective in its application of meaning and is produced not as a static, universal fact, but as discursive and contingent narratives. This representation of the Olympic Park site also operates simultaneously across three time zones – a temporal palimpsest of fiction and fact. The first is the moment the image occurs, capturing an imagined Olympic Games event colonised into the existing urban context (now denuded of content). The second moment is the representation several years hence, when the Games are reality. The third moment is the post-Games legacy – the promised land of regeneration. This legacy is utopian: a synthetic harmony of bioscience, healthy societies and augmented ecology *qua* the genetic code for regeneration. The legacy of the Olympic Games *is* the future, not just for the Lea Valley, but for all of London, all of England. Hybridised into a single representation is the existing site, the Olympic moment and the post-Olympic inhabitation. The image is thus a triple fantasy of the present as imagined, the Games as reality and the future as utopia.

Decoding the image: that which is represented never materialises, it is never translated 'as built'. But does it matter? Did anyone believe it anyway? The fantasy was expected, not the reality. Reality cannot live up to the image as the sky is never quite as blue, the grass as green nor the people quite so Stepford-ian. Paradoxically, reality is richer through the experience of lived space as haptic, sensual and phenomenological. The semiotic image cannot be totally controlled; people will add their own meanings and reinterpretations. The image remains a speculative hybrid of these multiple authors, viewers and users. But what remains of the image? Legacy. The promise of legacy was the dividing line between London's bid and the alternative cities' bids. 'Legacy' was not part of the requirements of the bid, nor was it considered by other cities, but it became the single deciding factor in London's success. The value of those six letters has been more than 9 billion of investment. The notion of legacy has already been translated into a statutory requirement in the consideration of major regeneration projects; that is, the promised utopia of cyber-sustainable, bio-urbanism. △D

Note
1. JL Borges, 'About William Beckford's Vathek' [1952], in *Other Inquisitions*, Washington Square Press (New York), 1966, p 146.

**Alejandro Zaera-Polo Architects/Foreign Office Architects,
2012 Olympics Masterplan, London, 2005**
The early Olympic vision. This image represents not reality,
nor even a future reality, but a utopian proposition.

Steven Tomlinson

David Kohn Architects, White Building Cultural Hub, Hackney Wick, London, 2011
A fringe strategy initiative to provide local residents with skills training, drawing on the talent of local artists while providing the artistic community with a public face – a place where local residents, artists and visitors co-exist in a beautiful setting on the very edge of the Olympic Park.

Slack space in an empty industrial site waiting for something to happen. The image is taken at Sugar House Lane and typifies post-industrial empty spaces in the Lea Valley.

CENTRING ON THE OLYMPIC FRINGE

Steven Tomlinson, a senior designer at the Olympic Park Legacy Company (OPLC), describes the challenges that exist post-Games in fully integrating the Olympic Park into the wider city's fabric and linking surrounding neighbourhoods with the site.

The Lea Valley once sat on the edge of London and on the periphery of the world's attention. Now that the London 2012 Olympic and Paralympic Games have created a renewed focus (and a huge development project) on the Lea, the challenge is to weave it into the city's fabric. The edge has become the new centre, and the Olympic Park a patch that needs to be stitched neatly into the wider context of London's East End, with a series of well-threaded projects.

The Lower Lea Valley is a largely brownfield area that represents a gap in London's intricate street pattern – what would appear on a map to be a large empty space. The introduction of the Games has created the potential to redress the industrial decline of the valley and provide a means for central government to invest in a way that would not otherwise have been achievable. The fact that large areas of the Lea have gone undeveloped for so many years is testament to the difficulty of the task. It has taken two back-to-back megaprojects – Westfield and the Olympic Park – to make the site inhabitable. The soil has been cleaned, rivers regulated, power lines diverted and many waterways bridged on an unprecedented scale. While the Olympic project has tackled the challenge head on, it has created a new fringe along the periphery of the development site, which in turn faces development pressure. The Olympic Park and surrounding areas are predicted to grow by up to around 30,000 homes in the next 20 years, 7,000 of which will be on the Olympic Park site. The main challenge faced in the fringe is to connect with both the wider districts and also into the Olympic Park. The very large event that is the Games will be inwardly focused and, although this will shift once over, the change will take time. The fringes need to prepare. Unlike the Games and the post-Games transformation, no single delivery agent is presently controlling that fringe. Thus the nature of what can be achieved is not imposed from above and can embody a degree of subtlety. The mayor's design agency, Design for London, sought to catch opportunities, obtain funding and steer projects while working with multiple public and private agencies through a set of simple principles: to connect, to value what is there and to create a mix. The aim is to link the surrounding neighbourhoods with the site. Nodes within the fringes are to become new centres or 'places of exchange'.

The Lea Valley's industrial and infrastructural past has created an engineered landscape entwined with a river valley of outstanding natural beauty. The network of rivers and canals, combined with major roads and railways, has created a series of unconnected urban islands. A century and a half of industrial peaks and troughs have left an abundance of derelict and slack spaces. Some lie empty, but East London has found unique ways of colonising these spaces; in many locations this adaptation has become a defining characteristic. Design for London has tried to draw on this natural creativity and work with those who have made these places their own to create projects that respond to local conditions.

The Olympic Fringe Delivery Strategy, a Design for London initiative now passed to the

30,000

NUMBER OF HOMES BY WHICH THE OLYMPIC PARK AND SURROUNDING AREAS ARE PREDICTED TO GROW IN THE NEXT 20 YEARS

Olympic Park Legacy Company (OPLC), is a comprehensive strategy funded by the Mayor of London delivering public realm, park and infrastructure improvements in the fringe.

Stratford Regional and International stations are well linked to the London transport system, but local routes into the Olympic Park, which will eventually be a community park as well as an international visitor destination, are sometimes sparsely populated, post-industrial, badly lit and difficult to navigate. Anxious to avoid the severed conditions to the north of Canary Wharf, the strategy employs a number of architects, landscape architects, artists and engineers to design and deliver a public realm framework that would improve the nature of these routes and encourage local ownership. In some cases improvements are made to local creations: a temporary intervention by an opportunistic local artist has been made into a permanent work; the active participation of community groups has been encouraged in tree planting. In other cases effort is focused on delivering important infrastructure.

This home-grown process is the inverse of the approach found on the inside of the fence; here the approach is to work closely with the detail of what currently exists while thinking strategically within the context of the bigger picture of development pressure. At a detailed level, street improvements alongside retailers located on strategic routes that will eventually lead into the Olympic Park are designed to encourage activity and stimulate the local economy. Other commissions include mapping businesses and

building uses in Hackney Wick, which has raised awareness of commercial and artistic activity in the area, created new networks and generated work for local entrepreneurs.

At a strategic level, Design for London has operated as a design adviser to the mayor, the boroughs and the London Thames Gateway Development Corporation. It has provided a detailed understanding of the area and sought to ensure connections and quality public realm are delivered through planning gain. The creation of conservation areas in Hackney Wick and Sugar House Lane have helped to preserve their industrial character and provide a context for future development – in the case of Sugar House Lane the network of yards and buildings, which emerged gradually over time, will help define a rich, mixed urban grain. These processes attempt to counterpoint the big-build tabula rasa approach.

The Lea River Park strategy won an International Urban Landscape Award for its vision for six new parks in the valley south of the Olympic Park. It finally realises Patrick Abercrombie's vision contained within the 1944 London Plan envisioning the Lea as the spine of regeneration in the east, creating a cohesive link from the Thames to the Olympic Park via a network of large open spaces for current and future developments. The Fatwalk towpath (so called due to its generous width and activity programme) is a route that connects these elements while delivering path infrastructure, land access rights, landscaping, a lift and a walkway through a 100-year-old bridge. These are required to complete the 42-kilometre

East Architecture/Urban Design, Leyton Links, Leyton, London, 2011
below left: Leyton High Road is the main link between Waltham Forest, Leyton station and the Olympic Park site. A series of carefully chosen enhancements on this important high street will improve the experience of the northeast side of the Park.

5th Studio Architects, Lea River Park, London, 2011
below right: A vibrant new 3.2-kilometre (2-mile) park is planned between the Olympic Park and the Thames. It will be brought forward in phases, will incorporate the listed gasholder sites as they are decommissioned, will open the site of the Abbey Mills Pumping Station, and make use of spoil from London's new subterranean rail line, Crossrail.

bottom left: Poplar Bridge, one of three new structures required to complete the Fatwalk – the linear park link through to Lea River Park from the Thames to the Olympic Park.

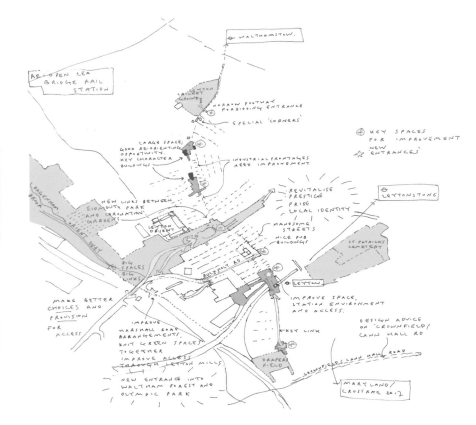

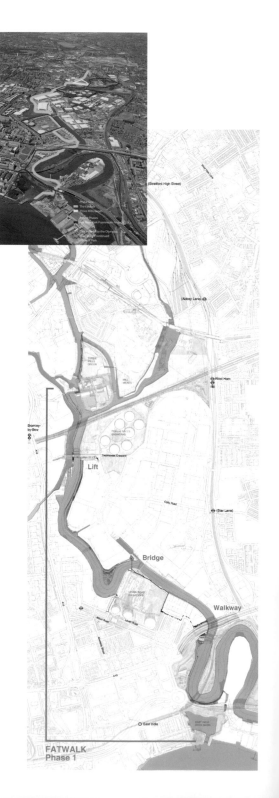

(26-mile) route from the Lea's source to the Thames.

Further fringe projects include proposals for Hackney Wick and Fish Island, Leyton Links, Hackney Marshes, Three Mills Green, Stratford High Street (part of High Street 2012) and Stratford town centre. Hackney Wick and Fish Island are sandwiched between London's busiest motorway (the A12) and the perimeter of the development zone for the Games. The few routes in, out and through the site are critical to its wider integration; however, its island nature and forgotten feel give the place a special character (defined by long-term residents, industrial buildings and an artist community) that one would seek to encourage rather than change. The Hackney Wick projects seek to soften the two major borders, by 'greening the grey' through tree planting alongside the highway and creating local amenities at the boundary of the development zone, and to provide ways into the Olympic Park, including two new bridges due to open after the Games, will link Hackney Wick with the Park. Work at Leyton focuses on improving physical and visual connections between key public zones, and providing a 'front door' to the Olympic Park with new pedestrian links over railway lines. Major public realm improvement projects are under way, which will see new green spaces, street furniture and lighting. Temporary uses are being encouraged to invigorate derelict shop frontages.

Hackney Marshes, often considered the spiritual home of grass-roots football, sits to the north of the Olympic Park, providing a reminder of the home-grown sporting history of the Lea. The ground, created from Second World War rubble, hosts more pitches in any one place than anywhere else in the world. The expansive flat field is highly active on a Sunday morning, but is mostly empty for the rest of the week. Football pitches have been consolidated and a range of other activities have been introduced; fishing platforms and a more diverse ecological landscape are planned for its edge, and a new changing facility and rooftop café established.

Though now peripheral to the big project it is the fringes that will be central to the outcome of the legacy of the London 2012 Olympic and Paralympic Games. By building on what is there and making it work for everyday life, the Lea Valley will be a place where ecology meets engineering, warehouse meets stadium, where a record-breaker's hotel accommodation is transformed into a family's living room; where residents can catch a train to Paris from their local station, where football meets fishing, and where industrial innovation works seamlessly with creative talent. With the right framework, it is possible to make this an extraordinary part of London. ⌂

Text © 2012 John Wiley & Sons Ltd. Images: p
102 © David Kohn Architects; pp 103, 104(l),
105(r) © Eleanor Fawcett; p 104(c) © ODA/
Anthony Charlton; pp 104(r), 105(;) © Design
for London; p 106(tl) © East Architecture/Urban
Design; p 106(tr) Courtesy of London Thames
Gateway Development Corporation and Steven
Tomlinson; p 106(bl&br) © 5th Studio Ltd; p
107(l&c) © Steven Tomlinson; p 107(l) © muf
architecture/art LLP

MJP Architects, Victoria Embankment
proposal, London, 2005
The widened pedestrian boulevard could
incorporate cafés, interpretation pavilions,
and exhibition or educational facilities.

Richard MacCormac evokes the Thames' defining relationship with London, as the boundary between north and south, the primacy of the north bank having remained almost unchallenged until the 21st century with the development of Tate Modern and the rejuvenation of the south bank.

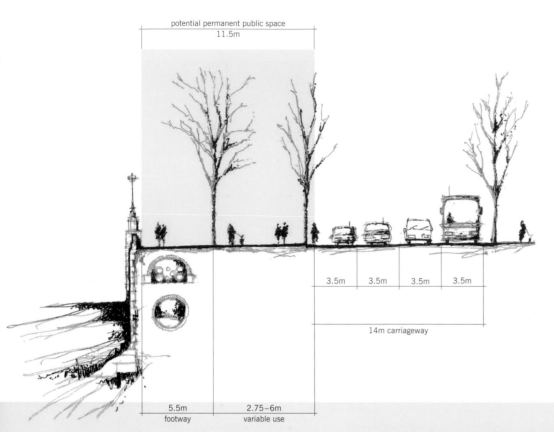

potential permanent public space
11.5m

3.5m   3.5m   3.5m   3.5m

14m carriageway

5.5m   2.75–6m
footway   variable use

It is peculiar that the Thames, unlike the rivers of other great cities such as Paris and Rome, has historically been London's southern boundary. This description is limited, of course, to the 'metropolitan' Thames – that stretch of river that unites the two cities on the north bank (the City of Westminster and the City of London) defined upstream by Westminster Bridge and downstream by Tower Bridge.

This gives the river a fundamental asymmetry that has affected how it has been developed and perceived. The north bank is characterised by the institutional territories of its hinterland – government, law and commerce – linked by the Victoria Embankment. Prior to the creation of that great thoroughfare the east–west route ran from the Royal Exchange through Cheapside, Ludgate Hill, Fleet Street, the Strand and Whitehall. This was historically (and still is) an amazingly rich urban mix which, in the 17th and 18th centuries, was characterised by vitality, criminality and vice, as recorded by Daniel Defoe (1661–1731) and William Hogarth (1697–1764), and most recently explored in Dan Cruickshank's *The Secret History of Georgian London*.[1] (The land between this artery and the Thames extended this milieu down to the river among gardens, great houses and institutions interspersed with the wharfs of commerce. Somerset House and the Adelphi stood with water gates at the river's edge.)

One admires Joseph Bazalgette's (1819–91) great thoroughfare as an engineering triumph, a single entity providing a sewer to end the stink of the Thames, a railway and a road linking the two cities. It is highly symbolic of London's status as a 19th-century world city. It is also, in a sense, very modern; it separates out the functions of transportation from the urban fabric with singular purpose, starting abruptly at Westminster and ending abruptly at Blackfriars. Its lateral connections are limited, particularly in relation to London's recreational quarter, Covent Garden, and strong connections to the Strand, occurring only twice – at Villiers Street and Essex Street. Victoria Embankment was not conceived for pleasure like a Parisian boulevard; it sanitised London's river frontage in moral contrast to the reputation of the Strand and Fleet Street.

Victoria Embankment was not conceived for pleasure like a Parisian boulevard; it sanitised London's river frontage in moral contrast to the reputation of the Strand and Fleet Street.

The 'buffer space' could be expanded at weekends to allow for exhibitions, festivals or demonstrations.

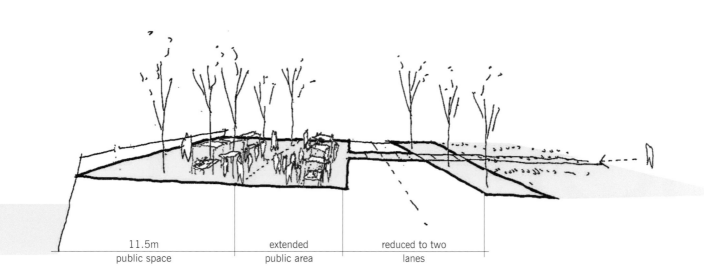

| 11.5m | extended | reduced to two |
| public space | public area | lanes |

The 'buffer space' could be expanded at weekends to allow for exhibitions, festivals or demonstrations.

Until the middle of the 18th century the south bank was undeveloped, apart from London's southern gateway at Southwark. During the 19th century it developed as part of London's hinterland of industry and docks, a landscape of cranes and wharfs, a context in which the symbolism of Tower Bridge appeared powerfully incongruous. The south bank's opportunities have been post-industrial and relatively recent in this stretch of river. County Hall placed London's government almost opposite the Palace of Westminster, and it is perhaps significant that the Greater London Authority (GLA) now finds itself opposite the Tower of London. The 1951 Festival of Britain projected the unlikely possibility that the south bank could become London's cultural quarter. This is, however, precisely how the site has grown up, with the Thames giving locational identity not just to the upriver South Bank complex, but to the downriver Design Museum, Globe Theatre and Tate Modern. Whereas the Victoria Embankment is Bazalgette's grand and finite proposition, the south bank is more like the pre-Bazalgette north, a series of serendipitous episodes. It is far more popular with Londoners as a place for strolling than the formal set piece opposite. These differences represent, perhaps, Danish architect and urban designer Jan Gehl's observation that the 19th-century city was about production while the 21st-century city would increasingly be recreational.

There are, nevertheless, opportunities on the north bank, which MJP Architects outlined to the London Development Agency (LDA) in 2005. The boulevard could be multimode – vehicular during the week and reduced to two lanes or, occasionally, total pedestrian use at weekends. Embankment Gardens could be opened up and stronger connections made between the Strand, Covent Garden, the Underground stations, riverboat services and floating facilities (which remain bleakly underdeveloped).

In contrast to the south bank, Victoria Embankment could be managed to provide an audience for the Thames as theatre, for great events, displays and carnivals. The thoroughfare itself could host functions, demonstrations and gatherings; kiosks and temporary buildings could shelter markets, fairs and festivals, and accommodate audiences for great parades. Schoolchildren could enjoy a tea party stretching from the Palace of Westminster to the Tower of London. ₪

Note
1. Dan Cruickshank, *The Secret History of Georgian London: How the Wages of Sin Shaped the Capital,* Random House (London), 2009.

SOME KEY FIGURES IN LONDON'S REGENERATI

A number of powerful individuals have played a significant role promoting regeneration in London. **Peter Murray** describes some of those who make up this important network of politicians, civil servants, planners and developers.

Nick Falk founded the URBED regeneration consultancy in 1976, soon after the ⚫ on London's Docklands. He currently focuses on town centres, suburbs and the reuse of redundant buildings.

In February 1975, ⚫ published a special issue under the title *Opportunity Docks*. Guest-editor **Nick Falk** invited a number of writers to comment on the future of the London Docks, an area of some 2,000 hectares (5,000 acres) – 50 times larger than the Covent Garden it area was the focus of considerable debate at the time. The scale of the docks is such that it must be the focus of any discussion about regeneration in London; few of those involved in the subject are untouched by it.

From the 1960s the docks had started to move downstream, as shipping moved towards containerisation and deeper waters, while related industries in East London were closing down. Falk, who was then researching the management of development at the London School of Economics (LSE) and actively involved in a number of community action groups, saw the redevelopment of the docks as a way of correcting the historic imbalance between the prosperous West End and poor East End and of housing the homeless.

Robert Maxwell's contribution to the ⚫ issue called on the planners to provide the infrastructure, but 'the actual building of the parts of the plan must be freed from pre-emptive decisions made on some central drawing board'. Frank Duffy (now Chair of the Stratford City Design Review Panel) called for the refurbishment of old warehouses into workspaces for crafts and tradesmen. Falk concluded with the comment: 'Anywhere in the third world this land would have been invaded by squatters quite able to organise their own patterns of settlement.'

Of course it did not happen like that. In 1981 the London Docklands Development Corporation (LDDC) was set up by the then Secretary of State for the Environment, Michael Heseltine. Heseltine is the most significant politician concerned with regeneration in Britain, first in generating the response to the inner-city riots of the early 1980s, and then in masterminding the successful City Challenge programme in the 1990s. The chief executive of the LDDC was Reg Ward who managed to get things moving after a series of failed proposals with an organically market-driven approach that chimed well with the Tory administration of the time. Significantly, the corporation was not provided with plan-making powers. Prime Minister Margaret Thatcher had little patience with planning. It was seen as a time-consuming activity which would not necessarily guarantee success, but which would instead inhibit rather than encourage early development.

Cover of Nick Falk's 1975 *Opportunity Docks* issue of ⚫.

Prime Minister Margaret Thatcher had little patience with planning. It was seen as a time-consuming activity which would not necessarily guarantee success, but which would instead inhibit rather than encourage early development.

Eric Sorensen was chief executive of the London Docklands Development Corporation (LDDC) from 1991 to 1997. He now runs Central London Forward, which makes the case for the capital's central area.

Regent's Canal, East London, 2011
top: Since much of the brownfield land in London is related to redundant Victorian infrastructure, regeneration areas frequently benefit from canals and industrial waterways. Developments that overlook water are much in demand.

Lea Valley, East London, 2011
The area around Stratford and the Olympic Park is threaded with waterways, many of which have suffered from half a century of neglect. The regeneration of this previously unrecognised asset is key to plans for lasting benefits after the London 2012 Olympic and Paralympic Games.

Ward was succeeded by a civil servant from the Inner Cities Directorate, **Eric Sorensen**, who provided a safe pair of hands for the burgeoning organisation. The LDDC built roads, housing, infrastructure, schools and the Docklands Light Railway. When it was closed down in 1998 it had invested £1.86 billion of public money to lever in £7.2 billion of private investment. If it failed, it was because of the lack of a physical plan; the piecemeal private development led to a paucity of place making and an inability to join the bits together to create a coherent metropolis. Sorensen went on to become Chairman of the Millennium Commission, whose regenerative exploits are a story of their own, and for a time was the chief executive of the Thames Gateway Partnership. What is now perceived as the Docklands' greatest success, Canary Wharf, was a piece of luck; the vision of a maverick American developer G Ware Travelstead, who saw the potential of providing large floor-plate buildings for the financial sector in the tax-light Enterprise Zone. Travelstead failed to raise the necessary funding and the project was taken over by the Reichman Brothers. As London's role as a global financial centre grew, Canary Wharf provided the space for the banking community that the City of London could not, thus ensuring London's pre-eminence in the European market.

The Docklands area forms part of the Thames Gateway, a concept promoted by Heseltine in the early 1990s. The idea of an eastern growth corridor came from Michael Simmons, who was then head of the London Planning Advisory Committee, a body set up after the demise of the Greater London Council (GLC) to provide strategic planning guidance. The thinking was that the completion of the Channel Tunnel Rail Link (CTRL) would fundamentally alter the transport geography of Europe, creating a development axis along the Thames estuary from the Medway towns and south Essex into London, to include Docklands.

While much has been done in the Thames Gateway through strategic physical and economic planning, as a concept it has lacked great popular support or gelled as an idea. Terry Farrell was responsible for the most compelling vision for the area when he suggested that the 200,000 homes proposed for the Gateway could be delivered in East London and the rest of the area turned into a national park. But the coalition government today is not taking a great interest in the Thames Gateway. Rather than supporting a strategic plan, it wants the people of the Thames Gateway to decide its future for themselves. Leadership will come from local authorities and the Mayor of London, building on Farrell's strategies. Such policies probably sound the death knell of the Gateway.

But regeneration is a slow job and happens incrementally. Thirty years after work started on replanning the Docks, vast tracts of the area still lay untouched and former Mayor of London Ken Livingstone decided to bid for the 2012 Olympic and Paralympic Games on the basis that it would regenerate this still impoverished district. Livingstone made clear that the regeneration of the East End would be the all-important legacy of the Games. His successor Boris Johnson has not deviated from that ambition. From September 2012, the Olympic Park Legacy Corporation (OPLC) will have powers to drive development in the area in much the same way as the LDDC did, although unlike the old corporation it will have plan-making powers. The OPLC will be formed from the current legacy company and it is likely that company chief executive, **Andrew Altman**, will head up the new organisation. His job will be to transform the Olympic Park into a new and thriving metropolitan area of the capital, reporting directly to the Mayor of London.

Altman is used to working with directly elected mayors. He came to London from Philadelphia where he had been Deputy Mayor for Planning and Economic Development and had previously worked for Anthony Williams in Washington DC, a mayor with a strong vision around urban planning. Altman's success is critical to the credibility of the London 2012 Games as an instrument for regeneration. While the OPLC will be responsible for putting the Olympic Park itself into public use and developing new family housing around it, it will have a wider remit of regeneration in the surrounding area, taking over responsibilities from other bodies including the London Thames Gateway Corporation.

One of the people Altman will work with is **Clive Dutton**, the charismatic head of regeneration, planning and property at Newham Council. Dutton brought a new energy to the borough when he arrived there in 2009 – just three years before the Games – from Birmingham City Council where he had been head of regeneration for the previous four years. Like Altman, he also brought the ability to work closely with an ambitious leader to deliver an effective regeneration programme. In the Midlands, Dutton worked closely with council leader Mike Whitby; now he is the facilitator for the strategies of Mayor of Newham Sir Robin Wales. His role is to ensure Newham maximises opportunities created not just by the 2012 Games, but also by Crossrail, London City Airport and Stratford International station.

Dutton's arrival has kick-started development in the troubled Royal Docks area with the signing of Siemens to build a pavilion that will be a permanent showcase for sustainable technologies and will be a flagship for the Green Enterprise District, which the mayor hopes will stretch across East London. Dutton's ability to get to grips with the Royal Docks was assisted by his professional empathy with Peter Bishop, who was then deputy chief executive of the London Development Agency (LDA), and Stephen Kennard, the head of property of the LDA, which owned most of the land.

Dutton's arrival has kick-started development in the troubled Royal Docks area with the signing of Siemens to build a pavilion that will be a permanent showcase for sustainable technologies and will be a flagship for the Green Enterprise District, which the mayor hopes will stretch across East London.

David Lunts, while at the Prince's Foundation, promoted the idea of the 'urban village', a concept that is now taking shape at Kidbrooke where he has worked closely with Berkeley Homes.

David Taylor, the 'godfather' of regeneration under New Labour, worked closely with the Deputy Prime Minister John Prescott while Labour was in office.

Both Dutton and Altman link up with **David Lunts**, interim director of housing and regeneration at the Greater London Authority (GLA) and formerly executive director for London at the Homes and Communities Agency. Like many of those involved in regeneration in the capital, Lunts began his regeneration career in the northwest and was Chair of Manchester City Council's Housing Committee from 1988 to 1995. He led the City Challenge renewal of Hulme before moving to London where he became chief executive of the Urban Villages Forum and the Prince's Foundation. He was then hired by the Office of the Deputy Prime Minister and worked closely with John Prescott. He was a member of Lord Rogers' Urban Task Force which promoted the concept of the compact city – ideas that were adopted by Ken Livingstone in the first London Plan. One of Lunts' key roles was to deliver Boris Johnson's promise of 50,000 affordable homes during his mayoralty. This, it seems, he will succeed in doing with the help of the government's Kickstart programme.

Another member of the 'Manchester mafia' is **David Taylor** who headed the regeneration arm of the construction company Amec, which was responsible for delivering the Hulme project. In 1993 he became the first chief executive of English Partnerships, where he pooled previously separate public grant and funding streams to target investment at areas of need. Today Taylor is a member of the Olympic Delivery Authority (ODA) board, while David Taylor Partnerships is involved in developing the former docks area at Canada Quays in Southwark, a joint venture with British Land. Taylor was less successful with the Royal Docks where he had hoped to build a masterplan by Terry Farrell for 4,900 homes, offices and retail, and an aquarium. But plans were scuppered by the collapse in residential values in 2008 and the LDA terminated its agreement with the developer.

GLC Architects Department, Ferrier Estate, Kidbrooke, London, 1972
The Ferrier Estate was a comprehensive development constructed using system building techniques. Poor management resulted in the deterioration of the physical and social fabric, leading to wholesale demolition. It is currently being transformed into Kidbrooke Village by Berkeley Homes.

Lifschutz Davidson Sandilands, Kidbrooke Village Masterplan, London, 2009–
Sir Bob Kerslake, Permanent Secretary at the Department for Communities and Local Government (centre with cup), David Lunts (centre) and Tony Pidgley, chairman of housebuilders the Berkeley Group, study the model of the Kidbrooke Village masterplan.

Chris Brown runs Igloo, an investment vehicle for regeneration projects in London and across the UK that focuses on sustainability and partnership with local communities.

Fred Manson first came to prominence when, as head of planning and regeneration at Southwark Council, he convinced Nick Serota to locate Tate Modern on Bankside.

Chris Brown was another who was involved with the Hulme project in Manchester. He is now the chief executive of Igloo, the regeneration arm of Morley Fund Management, the UK's first regeneration fund. Brown was also responsible for the development of Bermondsey Square in Southwark. While much of his other work has been outside London, Brown is a key member of the regeneration community, having been a member of the government's Urban Sounding Board, a director of the British Urban Regeneration Association (BURA), Chair of the Royal Institution of Chartered Surveyors (RICS) regeneration Panel, a Commission for Architecture and the Built Environment (CABE) Regional Design Ambassador, a member of the Prince's Foundation projects panel as well as writing a very popular blog for *Regeneration and Renewal* magazine. He is also part of the Bermondsey Neighbourhood Forum, one of 17 forums around the country that will test the workings of the new Localism Bill. The forum will develop Neighbourhood Plans in Bermondsey, an area focused on Bermondsey Square, a development by Igloo.

It would be hard to discuss the regeneration of Southwark without a mention of **Fred Manson**, now a director of Heatherwick Studios, but during the 1990s a very vocal and passionate head of planning and regeneration for the borough. It was during his watch that the Tate decided to locate its new home at Bankside that the More London project got moving and the Millennium Bridge was built. Southwark's relationship with the City of London, traditionally that of pauper and prince, was changed for ever. The regeneration of the north part of Southwark has been relatively swift; other areas like Elephant and Castle still struggle to come up with the right plans or the right money. Another long drawn-out saga is that of King's Cross.

Lifschutz Davidson Sandilands, City Point Townhouses, Kidbrooke Village, London, 2011
These simple affordable homes arranged as terraces with pitched roofs and a vernacular feel reference the same architects' seminal Coin Street housing project of 1994.

50,000

NUMBER OF AFFORDABLE HOMES PROMISED BY BORIS JOHNSON

Stanton Williams, Granary Building, King's Cross, London, 2011
The central section of the King's Cross masterplan, to the north of the Regent's Canal, includes the historic core of industrial architecture which has been converted to accommodation for the Central St Martins departments of the University of the Arts.

Roger Madelin is joint chief executive of Argent and responsible at King's Cross for one of Europe's largest regeneration projects.

In the late 1980s, Stuart Lipton's and Godfrey Bradman's London Regeneration Consortium hired Foster + Partners to masterplan the area around King's Cross and St Pancras station. The plans failed because of the property crash and little happened until, a decade ago, Argent put in a new bid for the site. **Roger Madelin**, the joint chief executive of Argent, is another major player who cut his teeth on delivering regeneration outside London. During the 1990s he developed Brindley Place in Birmingham. At King's Cross he undertook one of the most comprehensive programmes of consultation undertaken by any developer in the UK. Madelin himself publicly offered to speak to 'anyone at any time'. Nevertheless, it took until 2008 to get planning permission following a planning battle with Islington Council, in whose borough a small part of the site sits, and a judicial review following complaints by local community groups. All this despite the support of Peter Bishop,[1] who in the early days of the scheme was head of planning in Camden. The University of the Arts London moved into accommodation on the site in September 2011.

Stanton Williams, Granary Building, King's Cross, London, 2011
The Granary Building has been restored and re-engineered by Stanton Williams to provide accommodation for the University of the Arts London, the first major occupier to move into the new development.

RHWL and Richard Griffiths, St Pancras London Renaissance Hotel, St Pancras, London, 2011
George Gilbert Scott's remarkable Gothic edifice, the Midland Grand Hotel (1876), has been meticulously restored to provide a 245-bedroom hotel and 68 apartments for Harry Handelsman's Manhattan Lofts.

Allies and Morrison and Porphyrios Associates, King's Cross Masterplan, King's Cross, London, 2008–
As part of their engagement programme with the local community, the developers of King's Cross provide space on the site for 'meanwhile' uses such as this productive garden which is designed to move around the development as the construction programme permits.

The positive working relationship between Bishop and Madelin was of major significance in the development of the King's Cross masterplan and reflects a pattern found in many successful planning and regeneration projects where strong characters and relationships are essential to deliver effective change. The powerful figure of Sir Howard Bernstein, chief executive of Manchester City Council, has long been held as a model for the leadership of regeneration; it would seem that Andrew Altman's experience in the US of the close working relationship between elected mayors and planning officers has helped him to develop plans for lasting benefits after the Games in close consultation with Boris Johnson. Successful regeneration is as much about its leadership and relationships as it is about planning policies. In 1976, a year after editing the *D Opportunity Docks* issue, Nick Falk founded URBED, a consultancy specialising in urban regeneration and local economic development. He has been a leading intellectual force in the regeneration movement ever since, and is currently focused on the problems and regeneration of Outer London. *D*'s editors in the 1970s were keen supporters of self-help and community action, radical ideas that were anathema to the political establishment of the day. Rereading the *Docks* issue today, many of the propositions included in it would be well received by supporters of the Localism Bill that will soon become law. How strange it is to see ideas about planning and regeneration that once smacked of anarchy and leftism now being promoted by what is essentially a Tory government. *D*

The model of the masterplan is located in the German Gymnasium built in 1886, which houses the development's marketing suite as well as an event space that is loaned by the developers for community use.

Note
1. When Peter Bishop retired from his role as deputy chief executive of the London Development Agency (LDA) in April 2011, a large number of senior regeneration and development figures circulated their thoughts. Sir Stuart Lipton wrote: 'We will miss you. London needs you. From Tower Hamlets to Hammersmith to Camden to the LDA you have been a great inspiration and through your leadership some wonderful buildings and spaces have been produced.' Email from Sir Stuart Lipton to the author and others.

How strange it is to see ideas about planning and regeneration that once smacked of anarchy and leftism now being promoted by what is essentially a Tory government.

David Littlefield

ELEPHANT & CASTLE

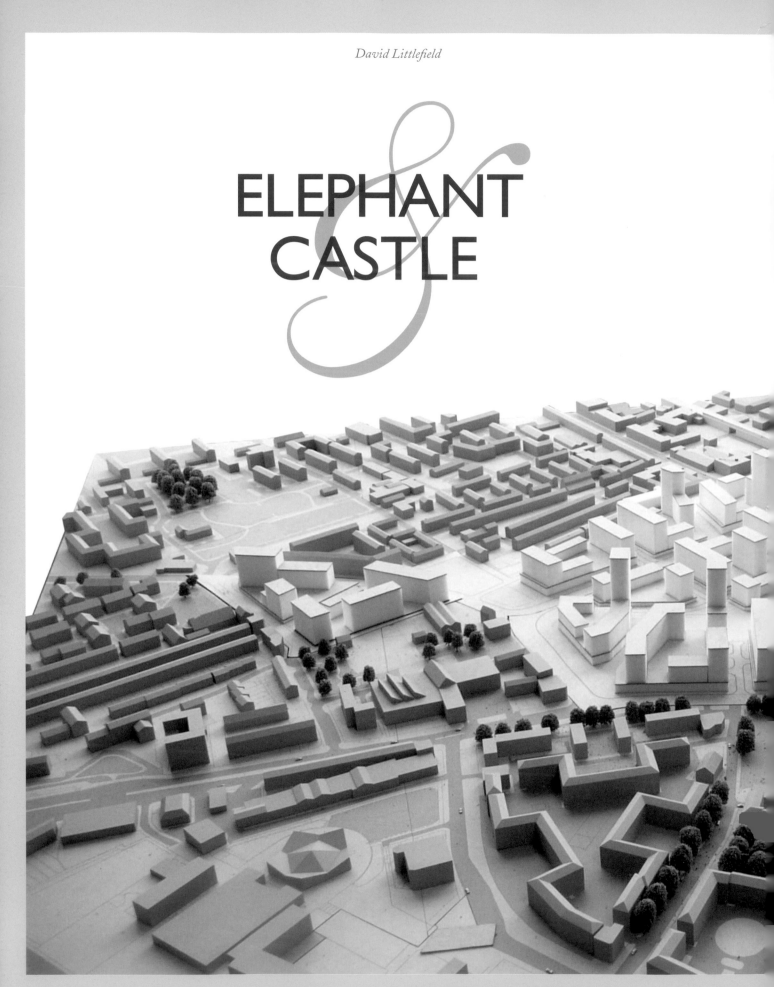

MAKE Architects, Elephant and Castle Masterplan, Elephant and Castle, London, 2010
Model illustrating the vision for an urban quarter of different building types, heights and massing. Building heights will increase towards the centre, while many residential units will be low-rise courtyard designs.

Located south of the river, Elephant and Castle is sited within a bend in the Thames that enables it to function as a significant transport node and puts it within quick and easy reach of significant destinations such as Westminster, Victoria and London Bridge. By the 1940s, however, the area had become characterised by poverty and slum housing, and a 1946 plan for urban renewal paved the way for large slab blocks and expressways that emerged over succeeding decades. Following Modernist ideals of elevated living, the separation of pedestrians and traffic, and repetitive housing units, Elephant and Castle came to exemplify postwar dreams gone wrong: ill-lit underpasses, poor construction, an urban realm of impermeability and a general sense of alienation. Since the late 1990s the London Borough of Southwark has planned for the Elephant's renewal, and the wider London Plan drawn up by the mayor's office includes the area as a zone with the capacity to meet the city's need for new homes and jobs. In order to manage such a large, complex and ambitious programme (which, as a 'living' part of the city, cannot be sealed off and rebuilt like the Olympic Park site) the local authority has divided the area into distinct territories. There is an overarching Opportunity Area of 69 hectares (170 acres) which, according to version 16 of the Master Regeneration Plan published in June 2010, plans for: 'a thriving and successful mixed-use major town centre that is safe, full of vitality and accessible to and from a highly integrated public transport system; combining historic character with a high-quality design and layout of new buildings; a place where people will want to live, work and visit for shopping and leisure.'[1]

Within the Opportunity Area is a smaller Core Area of 25 hectares (62 acres). Within this core, Southwark plans to build 4,000 new homes, 45,000 square metres (484,376 square feet) of new shopping and leisure space, and between 25,000 and 30,000 square metres (269,097 and 322,917 square feet) of business space, as well as initiating public realm improvements such as enhanced lighting, park space and improved connectivity across the site. The 43-storey, 148-metre (485-foot) high Strata Tower is the most visible alteration within the Core Area, although the 408-apartment building (the tallest residential tower in the city) is not without its critics – it was dismissed by the *Daily Telegraph* as 'quite simply the worst tall building ever constructed in London' when completed in 2010.[2]

The lion's share of the Core Area is now the subject of a more focused masterplanning exercise by MAKE Architects on behalf of Lend Lease, which signed a regeneration agreement with Southwark in 2010. Comprising the replacement of the slab housing blocks of the large Heygate Estate and a smaller site at Rodney Road, as well as negotiations over the indoor shopping mall, the emerging masterplan aims to reinstate something approaching the prewar street pattern and to introduce a range of buildings to attract a wider cross-section of society. 'This is a failed estate – a failed place in terms of what a real community should be. It was very much mono-tenure and didn't connect with the communities around it,'

Ownership diagram. Land under public ownership is depicted in green. Such a large amount of public land makes decision taking and consultation more efficient, but key sites – such as the retail mall in the centre – are under private control.

Green spaces. As well as illustrating the new street pattern and major routes for connectivity across the site, this image emphasises the proposal for new green spaces, presently sorely lacking.

North–south connectivity. The main 'public face' and vehicular hub of the Elephant is highlighted in the red circle; the need for a strong north–south route, negotiating the railway line, is indicated by the red arrow.

THE EMERGING MASTERPLAN AIMS TO REINSTATE SOMETHING APPROACHING THE PREWAR STREET PATTERN AND TO INTRODUCE A RANGE OF BUILDINGS TO ATTRACT A WIDER CROSS-SECTION OF SOCIETY.

ELEPHANT & CASTLE

says Lend Lease project director Rob Deck. What we've got are buildings which have no regard for the grid of streets or patterns of community which existed prior to it.'[3]

Current plans, which were the subject of widespread consultation during summer 2011, propose to create stronger east–west and north–south links, and, using a wide range of architects (perhaps a dozen or more), to design a mixed neighbourhood that places a premium on variety, connectivity and safety. Around 2,500 residential units are planned, with active frontages comprising street-level retail and office premises to encourage a sense of ownership and natural surveillance. An outline masterplan for the large Heygate Estate is due to be submitted during spring 2012, along with a detailed plan for the smaller Rodney Road site, which has already been demolished. The programme is envisaged to be complete within 15 years. △

Notes
1. See http://moderngov.southwarksites.com/(S(ubcqgt45u3vkwp55m3eziojf))/ mgConvert2PDF.aspx?ID=10890.
2. *Daily Telegraph*, 12 August 2010; www.telegraph.co.uk/property/propertynews/7940897/Strata-tower-in-Elephant-and-Castle-named-ugliest-new-building-of-the-year.html.
3. Telephone interview between Rob Deck and the author, 6 July 2011.

WORKS
IN/ON//AROU

Hilary Powell, **Still from** ***The Games*, Optimistic Productions, 2007**
opposite: Event: Hubcap discus. Location: South of Greenway/Northern Outfall Sewer dissecting the future London 2012 Olympic Park. Filmed in 2007, *The Games* staged a DIY Olympics amid the sites and communities that would soon be making way for the construction of the Park. As a creative intervention in, and playful critique of, tabula rasa urbanism, the film acted as a celebration, swansong and document of an area undergoing dramatic change.

ND /// BEHIND PROGRESS

Artist **Hilary Powell** describes how her work in film, food and the pop-up book offers playful critiques of regeneration and place making.

The Games (2007) staged a surreal DIY Olympics amid the sites and communities to be erased within the Demolish Dig Design phase of the London 2012 Olympic and Paralympic Games. As the Olympic machine declared this area of East London a dirty/blank space on the map, it became imperative to construct a counter-narrative that responded to, celebrated and captured the 'now-time' of the area, questioning the rhetoric of erasure and grand narrative of progress inherent in such large-scale regeneration projects – particularly one with the powerful utopian ideology of the Olympic Games behind it. The mega event became a rich and immediate source material – from its iconography (a playful subversion of Leni Riefenstahl's film of the 1936 Berlin Games) to its history (London's 1948 'austerity' Games and ethos of making do/getting by).

Shot over two freezing weekends in February 2007, the film-making became a lesson in disappearances: streets closed overnight, and our makeshift sporting arenas shifted with ever-advancing security fences. What had been our Wild East was now the Last Chance Saloon, the swansong of an area on the brink of dramatic change as ailing athletes trampled through/over contested territories. Acquired by the British Film Institute (BFI) and archived within the Museum of London (MoL), the film became part of a layered and collected history of the area. Homage, intervention and critique, its momentary rupture in use and value is part of the memory of an obliterated and repackaged site.

In July 2007, the Olympic Delivery Authority (ODA) took possession of the site; streets that played key roles in The Games became off limits. But other routes, literal and imaginative, opened up, and other sources were ripe for the picking. Pacing overgrown canalsides and the edgeland territory of the blue fence became a pathway to the past and a way of weaving fact and fiction. Pudding Mill River: Purveyors of Sporting Spirits and Foodstuffs was born of the abundance of wild,

Hilary Powell, 'The Critical Pop-Up Book: Re-Imagining London's
Olympic Structures of Enchantment', Bartlett School
of Architecture, University College London (UCL), 2011
opposite and previous page: Pop-up work in progress. Hanging
files, photographic images, video projection. The project is part of a
three-year Arts & Humanities Research Council (AHRC) Fellowship
in the Creative and Performing Arts based at the Bartlett School of
Architecture, UCL.

Pudding Mill River: Purveyors of Sporting
Spirits and Foodstuffs, Olympic Park
fringelands, London, 2008
Pudding Mill River hard at work harvesting
next to the Olympic Park's blue fence.
Pudding Mill River: Purveyors of Sporting
Spirits and Foodstuffs are gathering the
last wild harvests of the Olympic zone
and creating and branding delicious
vintages with some extra-special Olympian
properties.

2

NUMBER OF WEEKENDS
DURING WHICH POWELL'S
THE GAMES
WAS FILMED

edible growth fringing the Olympic Park site
– elderflower boughs blocking pathways, wild
roses furtively traversing barriers. And what
if the spirit of an area could be bottled and
valued as a precious vintage, in the same way
as the canned 'last breath of communism'
or packaged pieces of the Berlin Wall? Sloe
Lea Gin (a distillation of this elusive essence)
is the defining product in the firm's range.
Thriving on resilient local harvests, Pudding
Mill River, and its entrepreneurial guerrilla
gatherers, aligns itself with the history of
other local industries (Yardley soap, Clarnico
sweets) and builds its brand narrative from a
potent blend of myth and reality.

Each project finds a precarious,
imaginative, questioning way through, behind
and beyond the masterplan. Choreographic
scenographies, myth making and spatial
narratives form a history of inhabitation
and intervention in this shifting landscape;
the gathered material creates an accidental
archive of place that models the dynamics of
urban change.

*And what if the spirit of an area
could be bottled and valued as
a precious vintage, in the same
way as the canned 'last breath of
communism' or packaged pieces
of the Berlin Wall? Sloe Lea Gin
(a distillation of this illusive
essence) is the defining product
in the firm's range.*

In their association with the Gothic
structures of fairy tales, pop-up books have
been described as 'structures of enchantment'.
Drawing on a tradition of 'romantic ruinology'
(depicting the centres of power as ruins),
'The Critical Pop-up Book: Re-Imagining
London's Olympic Structures of Enchantment'
appropriates pop-up and other movable
book forms to critique mythic narratives of
regeneration – in themselves such 'structures
of enchantment'. The structural transformation
involved in each animated page stages
urban processes of progress and entropy –
manifestations of the artist Robert Smithson's
concept of 'ruins in reverse' in which buildings
rise into ruin as they are built. The project is a
reaction to, and subversion of, utopian legacy
images; as urban quarters are branded and
old street names give way to new, a complex,
layered vista of time and space in London's
Lower Lea Valley opens up. ⌂

Andrea Arnold, *Fish Tank*, 2009
In Arnold's extraordinary film we encounter the
landscapes of Rainham on the London/Essex
border experienced largely through the eyes of
15-year old Mia (played by Katie Jarvis).

WHERE

In the last few decades, the
boundaries of London have
become difficult to demarcate
with intense urbanisation and
increasing pressure on the
green belt. **Matthew Gandy**
explores the significance of
the city's fringe and its 'edge'
landscapes.

DOES

How do we know we have reached the edge of the city? Is it an aluminium sign? Is it a thinning-out of buildings until there is little but woods and fields? Or is it an abrupt shift to small towns and villages dotted across the landscape? Perhaps it is really none of these things since the city, or at least 'urbanisation', is now practically everywhere. In his book *The Urban Revolution*, first published in 1970, the French urbanist Henri Lefebvre makes a clear distinction between 'city' and 'urbanisation'. 'Society has become completely urbanised,' he writes, 'This urbanisation is virtual today, but will become real in the future'.[1]

In the 40 years since Lefebvre wrote these words, the pace and scale of urban growth has accelerated and so has the more ubiquitous dynamic of 'urbanisation', as infrastructure and ideas have spread into the remotest locales. The urban and the rural have become increasingly difficult to differentiate despite the powerful cultural resonance of this distinction. We can never really understand cities as simply 'things in themselves' since they are manifestations of broader processes of change, connection and recombination. Cities are just a particular form of urbanisation.

If we consider London, its current metropolitan boundaries were created in 1965. For the purposes of data collection, planning and service provision these administrative boundaries are extremely significant, but they reveal only part of the story of what London is as a cultural and geographical entity. If we look within these 'lines on the map' where London's outer boroughs meet the ring of counties stretching from Kent in the southeast,

THE

through the affluent commuter belt of Surrey, Buckinghamshire and Hertfordshire, to Essex in the northeast, we find that the distinction between London and 'not London' is hazy in terms of identity and topography. A closer look at the 1:25,000 Ordnance Survey map of where the outer London borough of Enfield meets the county of Hertfordshire reveals the complexity of the northern edge of the city: a jumble of archaeological sites, allotments, copses, farms, golf courses, housing estates, playing fields, infrastructure installations and other features. And just a few hundred metres further north is the constant rumble of the M25 motorway that Iain Sinclair followed as his walking route around the city in *London Orbital*.[2]

At or beyond the urban fringe, especially in the east of London, we find spaces of intense marginalisation that alter the more familiar map of inner-city deprivation. In Andrea Arnold's extraordinary film *Fish Tank* (2009), for example, we encounter the working-class landscapes of Rainham on the London/Essex border. Arnold not only reveals a profound sense of social and cultural claustrophobia, but also the striking significance of 'edge' landscapes that veer between an oppressive sense of utilitarian functionality and moments of striking revelation through encounters with 'wild urban nature'.

The green-tinged edge of London is artificially sustained, however, by the 'green belt', a planning device that was first mooted in the mid-1930s and then introduced in the early 1960s in order to prevent ribbon development, sprawl and the drift

CITY

Purfleet, Thurrock, Essex
Purfleet is a predominantly white working-
class community on the edge of London
in the ultra-marginal parliamentary
constituency of Thurrock.

towards total urbanisation in which only pockets of open space might have remained.[3] More recently, the green belt has come under intense development pressure from all directions: it is threatened by the ideological assault on strategic planning as an restrictive anachronism, but is also challenged as an impediment to the production of new homes that further inflates the London housing market. The real relationship, however, between regional planning, housing and development across London is more complex than these polarised debates would suggest, but there remains intense local resistance to any widespread modification of the green belt. Spaces beyond London's green belt are now being drawn into 'zones of intensification' through the extension of transport infrastructure such as the east–west Crossrail behemoth under construction or the earmarking of immense areas such as the so-called Thames Gateway to the east as arenas for state-facilitated development – in the case of the Gateway, despite its remoteness and vulnerability to future flooding.

In addition to roads and other transport infrastructure such as airports, the physical reach of London is also marked by more complex, distant and less widely understood networks. These range from the 'soft landscapes' of communications to the vast technological systems that provide energy and water for the city. In the case of water supply, London has extensive network of pipes, pumping stations, reservoirs, treatment plants and other infrastructure that is largely unseen and unnoticed by most of the city's inhabitants: only in moments of crisis or failure do these

END

complex and vulnerable systems come sharply into public view.

And what of London's global imprint? Some social scientists and urban ecologists have sought to measure the impact of cities through concepts such as the 'ecological footprint' and other indicators of the environmental effects of urban consumption. In the case of London, the aggregate impact of the city is immense, yet per capita contributions reveal more local differences and anomalies: poorer parts of the city, for example, have a significantly lower environmental impact because of less car ownership as well as lower levels of consumption, long-haul travel and other factors. Similarly, if we explore per capita environmental impact at a regional or national level there are affluent rural or semi-rural communities that blur the conceptual utility of the 'city' as a focus for environmental anxiety. If we disentangle the metaphorical and ideological aspects of the environmental critique of cities, it becomes possible to focus on the urban process as a socio-environmental dynamic that transcends the often arbitrary distinctions between the city and the 'non-city'. And if we move our attention from the material dimensions of urban space to less tangible or visible threads of connection such as cultural networks, financial transactions and other elements, then what we understand London to be becomes immeasurably more complex, diffuse and pervasive. △D

Rainham Marshes, Essex
Rainham Marshes is a former military firing range that was opened to the public as a nature reserve for the first time in 2006. It is located at the eastern edge of London, adjacent to the Thames estuary in Purfleet, Thurrock and Havering.

Notes
1. Henri Lefebvre, *The Urban Revolution*, University of Minnesota Press (Minneapolis, MN), 2003 [1970].
2. Iain Sinclair, *London Orbital*, Granta (London), 2002.
3. David Thomas, 'London's Green Belt: The Evolution of an Idea', *The Geographical Journal* 129 (1), March 1963, pp 14–24.

Michael Batty is Bartlett Professor of Planning at University College London (UCL) where he manages the Centre for Advanced Spatial Analysis (CASA). He has worked on computer models of cities since the 1970s with a strong emphasis on using such tools to inform the planning process through state-of-the-art visualisation. He is editor of *Environment and Planning B* and his most recent book is *Cities and Complexity* (MIT Press, 2005). He is a Fellow of the Royal Society and was appointed a CBE for services to geography in 2005. His website (www.complexCity.info) provides a glimpse of his work.

Peter Bishop trained in town planning at Manchester University and has spent his entire career working in London. Over the past 25 years he has been a planning director in four different Central London boroughs and has worked on major projects including Canary Wharf, the development of the BBC's campus at White City and the King's Cross development. In 2006 he was appointed as the first director of Design for London, the mayor's architecture and design studio. He is an adviser to the Mayor of London and a director at the architectural firm Allies and Morrison-Urban Practitioners. He lectures and teaches extensively, is a visiting professor at the Faculty of Architecture and the Built Environment at the Nottingham Trent University, an Honorary Fellow of UCL and an Honorary Fellow of the Royal Institute of British Architects (RIBA).

Matthew Carmona is Professor of Planning and Urban Design at the Bartlett School of Planning at UCL. His research has focused on processes of design governance and the policy context for delivering better-quality built environments. His background is as an architect and a planner and he has published widely in the areas of urban design, design policy and guidance, housing design and development, measuring quality and performance in planning, on the management of public space and on public space and design in London.

Edward Denison is an independent consultant, writer and architectural photographer. He recently completed an AHRC-funded PhD in architectural history at the Bartlett School of Architecture, UCL, where he is a teaching Fellow. His international work concentrates on the built enironment, culture and change, and can be explored at www.denisonren.com. His books include: *Asmara: Africa's Secret Modernist City* (Merrell, 2003), *Building Shanghai* (Wiley, 2006), *Modernism in China* (Wiley, 2008), *McMorran & Whitby* (RIBA, 2009) and *The Life of the British Home* (Wiley, 2012).

Mike Devereux is a senior lecturer in the Department of Planning & Architecture, University of the West of England, Bristol. After reading geography and civic design at university he gained 10 years' experience in practice. His research interests focus on the design of built environments, in particular historical and international comparisons of place and the different roles that planning has to play in shaping them.

Sir Terry Farrell CBE is considered to be the UK's leading architect planner, with offices in London and Hong Kong. During 40 years in practice he has completed many award-winning buildings and masterplans, including Embankment Place and the Home Office headquarters, as well as millennium projects such as The Deep in Hull and the Centre For Life in Newcastle. UK masterplans include Greenwich Peninsula, Paddington Basin and Newcastle Quayside. Throughout his career he has championed urban planning and helped shape government policy on key issues. In London, he is design adviser to the mayor, and advises the Department for Transport on high-speed rail. He is design champion for the Thames Gateway, Europe's largest regeneration project, and masterplanner for the transformation of Holborn and Earl's Court in London.

Murray Fraser is Professor of Architecture and Global Culture at the Bartlett School of Architecture, UCL. His book (with Joe Kerr) on *Architecture and the 'Special Relationship': The American Influence on Post-War British Architecture* (Routledge, 2007) won the RIBA President's Research Award and Bruno Zevi Book Prize. As a qualified architect, he has jointly set up the Palestinian Regeneration Team. He chairs the RIBA Research Committee, sits on the RIBA Awards Group, and co-edits *The Journal of Architecture*.

Matthew Gandy is a professor of geography at UCL and was director of the UCL Urban Laboratory from 2006 to 2011. His publications include: *Concrete and Clay: Reworking Nature in New York City* (MIT Press, 2002), *Hydropolis* (Campus, 2006) and *Urban Constellations* (Jovis, 2011), along with articles in *New Left Review*, *International Journal of Urban and Regional Research*, *Urban Studies* and many other journals. He is also actively involved in local issues in Hackney, East London, and is a member of Hackney Biodiversity Partnership and Hackney Environment Network.

Robert Harbison has taught at the Architectural Association (AA) in London and at London Metropolitan University. He is the author of *Eccentric Spaces* (MIT Press, 2000), *Reflections on Baroque* (Reaktion Books, 2002) and, most recently, *Travels in the History of Architecture* (Reaktion Books, 2009) among others.

Hattie Hartman is an American architect and journalist and has been based in London since 1991. She holds an undergraduate degree in fine arts (architectural history) from Harvard University and a joint Masters in architecture and urban studies from MIT. She has worked as an architect in three capitals – Brasilia, Washington DC and London – and began working as a freelance journalist in 1998. In 2006 she joined *The Architects' Journal* as technical editor and took on the newly created role of sustainability editor in 2008. She is the author of the book *London 2012: Sustainable Design – Delivering an Olympic Legacy* (John Wiley & Sons, 2011).

Sir Richard MacCormac CBE founded MJP Architects in 1972 and has now established a separate practice, MacCormac Architect. As well as being a committed practitioner working in historic contexts with projects that include buildings for Trinity College, Cambridge, and St John's College, Oxford, he has taught and lectured widely and published numerous articles on urban design, architectural theory and history. He is a Royal Academician and served as President of the RIBA from 1991 to 1993. He is currently an adviser to the historic City of Bath.

Peter Murray trained at Bristol and the AA before joining ⌂ under Monica Pidgeon (1970–4). He was then variously editor of *Building Design*, editor of *RIBA Journal* and co-founder and publisher of *Blueprint* magazine. He is currently founder chairman of the New London Architecture centre, chairman of Wordsearch and founder director of the London Festival of Architecture.

Hilary Powell is AHRC Fellow in the creative and performing arts at the Bartlett School of Architecture, UCL. Her interdisciplinary practice consistently engages with, and intervenes in, sites of urban transformation. Her film *The Games* (2007) led to sustained work around the London 2012 Olympic and Paralympic Games project and a series of events called the Salon de Refuse Olympique. She is now editing a book examining critical creative responses to the 2012 Games (Myrdle Court Press, April 2012).

Louis Rice is an architect and spent over a decade in practice in France and the UK. For the last five years he has worked as a senior research fellow and senior lecturer at the University of the

West of England in Bristol, as head of urban design, and runs the MArch design studio. His research interests include informal urbanism, play and transgression.

Steven Tomlinson is a senior designer at the Olympic Park Legacy Company (OPLC), responsible for design, planning and delivery of the Olympic Park legacy. He previously worked at Design for London and Transport for London, and is a visiting lecturer at the University of Westminster.

Austin Williams is the director of Future Cities Project Ltd and lecturer in architecture at Xi'an Jiaotong-Liverpool University in Suzhou, China. He is a chartered architect, film producer and journalist and was previously the technical editor at *The Architects' Journal* and transport correspondent with the *Daily Telegraph*. He is an independent programme-maker, writer and illustrator of *Shortcuts* (RIBA, 2008 and 2009), and co-editor of *The Lure of the City: From Slums to Suburbs* (Pluto Press, 2011) and *The Future of Community: Reports of a Death Greatly Exaggerated* (Pluto, 2008).

INDIVIDUAL BACKLIST ISSUES OF △ ARE
AVAILABLE FOR PURCHASE AT £22.99 / US$45

TO ORDER AND SUBSCRIBE SEE BELOW

What is Architectural Design?

Founded in 1930, *Architectural Design* (△) is an influential and prestigious publication. It combines the currency and topicality of a newsstand journal with the rigour and production qualities of a book. With an almost unrivalled reputation worldwide, it is consistently at the forefront of cultural thought and design.

Each title of △ is edited by an invited guest-editor, who is an international expert in the field. Renowned for being at the leading edge of design and new technologies, △ also covers themes as diverse as: architectural history, the environment, interior design, landscape architecture and urban design.

Provocative and inspirational, △ inspires theoretical, creative and technological advances. It questions the outcome of technical innovations as well as the far-reaching social, cultural and environmental challenges that present themselves today.

For further information on △, subscriptions and purchasing single issues see: www.architectural-design-magazine.com

How to Subscribe

With 6 issues a year, you can subscribe to △ (either print or online), or buy titles individually.

Subscribe today to receive 6 issues delivered direct to your door!

INSTITUTIONAL SUBSCRIPTION
£230 / US$431 combined print & online

INSTITUTIONAL SUBSCRIPTION
£200 / US$375 print or online

PERSONAL RATE SUBSCRIPTION
£120 / US$189 print only

STUDENT RATE SUBSCRIPTION
£75 / US$117 print only

To subscribe:
Tel: +44 (0) 1243 843272
Email: cs-journals@wiley.com

Volume 80 No 5
ISBN 978 0470 744987

Volume 80 No 6
ISBN 978 0470 746622

Volume 81 No 1
ISBN 978 04707 47209

Volume 81 No 2
ISBN 978 0470 748282

Volume 81 No 3
ISBN 978 0470 664926

Volume 81 No 4
ISBN 978 0470 686806

Volume 81 No 5
ISBN 978 0470 669884

Volume 81 No 6
ISBN 978 0470 689790